Ireon

Bookmarks
London, Chicago and Melbourne

Ireland's permanent revolution

Chris Bambery

Ireland's permanent revolution / *Chris Bambery*
Third edition February 1990.
First published April 1986, second edition December 1987.
Bookmarks, 265 Seven Sisters Road, London N4 2DE, England
Bookmarks, PO Box 16085, Chicago, IL 60616, USA
Bookmarks, GPO Box 1473N, Melbourne 3001, Australia
Copyright © Bookmarks and Chris Bambery

ISBN 0 906224 55 1

Printed by Cox and Wyman Limited, Reading, England
Cover design by Peter Court

Bookmarks is linked to an international grouping of socialist organisations:
Australia: *International Socialists*, GPO Box 1473N, Melbourne 3001
Belgium: *Socialisme International*, Rue Lovinfosse 60, 4030 Grivegnée
Britain: *Socialist Workers Party*, PO Box 82, London E3
Canada: *International Socialists*, PO Box 339, Station E, Toronto,
        Ontario M6H 4E3
Denmark: *Internationale Socialister*, Ryesgade 8, 3, 8000 Århus C
France: *Socialisme International*, BP 189, 75926 Paris Cedex 19
Greece: *Organosi Sosialistiki Epanastasi*, PO Box 8161, 10010 Omonia,
        Athens.
Holland: *Groep Internationale Socialisten*, PO Box 9720, 3506 GR Utrecht
Ireland: *Socialist Workers Movement*, PO Box 1648, Dublin 8
Norway: *Internasjonale Sosialister*, Postboks 5370, Majorstua, 0304 Oslo 3
United States: *International Socialist Organization*, PO Box 16085,
        Chicago, IL 60616
West Germany: *Sozialistische Arbeiter Gruppe*, Wolfgangstrasse 81, 6000
        Frankfurt 1

This book is published with the aid of the Bookmarks Publishing Co-operative. Many socialists have some savings put aside, probably in a bank or savings bank. While there, this money is being loaned out by the bank to some business or other to further the capitalist search for profit. We believe it is better loaned to a socialist venture to further the struggle for socialism. That's how the co-operative works: in return for a loan, repayable at a month's notice, members receive free copies of books published by Bookmarks. At the time this book was published, the co-operative had 400 members, from as far apart as London and Malaysia, Canada and Norway. Since 1980, the co-operative has helped publish fifty books.

Like to know more? Write to the Bookmarks Publishing Co-operative, 265 Seven Sisters Road, Finsbury Park, London N4 2DE, England.

Acknowledgements
Many people have helped in preparing this book. Particular thanks are due
to Kieran Allen, Alex Callinicos, Lindsey German, Chris Harman, Peter
Marsden, Pat Stack and Steve Wright.
Chris Bambery, December 1989

Chris Bambery is a member of the Socialist Workers Party
in Britain. He writes regularly for the weekly paper **Socialist Worker**
and the monthly **Socialist Worker Review**.

Contents

Northern Ireland

Introduction

AT FIVE O'CLOCK on the afternoon of 14 August 1969 British troops moved into position around the Bogside area of Derry. For the previous three days the population of this Catholic working-class ghetto had been besieged by the armed police of the Royal Ulster Constabulary, the RUC, and the B-Specials, the police reserve, also armed. The RUC had saturated the area with tear-gas and made innumerable baton-charges. The people of the Bogside had responded with stones and petrol-bombs. They had fought the RUC to a standstill.

The Battle of the Bogside was the high-point of a rising level of violence in Northern Ireland. For twelve months civil rights marchers had been demanding an end to discrimination, unemployment and bad housing. For twelve months the RUC, supported by Protestant mobs, had answered them with baton-charges and water-cannon.

According to the British government the troops were now being sent in to protect the Catholic population. The then Labour government hurriedly assured everyone that the army was there to keep the peace and preserve civil rights.

In private Labour politicians were more honest. James Callaghan, the home secretary who ordered the troops to be sent in, later recalled in his book **A House Divided**:

> When I got back to the Home Office I was informed that earlier in the afternoon Sir Harold Black, the secretary to the Northern Ireland Cabinet, had telephoned to say that Anthony Peacocke, the Inspector-General, feared that the police would be unable to contain the Bogside for much longer and that if troops were not made available the police

would be compelled to retreat from their position in front of the barricades.

The troops were being sent in to back up the RUC and prevent defeat for the forces of 'law and order'. Yet at the very moment that troops began to arrive in Derry, those same 'forces of law and order', the RUC and B-Specials, were leading a Protestant mob in an all-out assault on the Catholic Lower Falls area of Belfast. The RUC opened up on unarmed civilians with machine-guns mounted on armoured cars. Over two nights, eight people died, 500 Catholic homes were burnt out and 1500 families forced to flee the area.

For fifty years Britain had presided over a state created in Northern Ireland to ensure a political majority for the Unionist Party; a state in which Catholics were second-class citizens, discriminated against in jobs, housing and education; a state whose security was guaranteed by an armed all-Protestant police force and by repressive laws that had won the admiration of the racist rulers of apartheid South Africa.

Now, back in London, the Labour government was discussing its attitude to the demands by Catholics for civil rights. Home secretary James Callaghan and defence minister Denis Healey spelt out the policy that their successors, both Labour and Tory, would follow. As one of their cabinet colleagues, Richard Crossman, noted in his diary: 'Callaghan and Healey both reminded us that our whole interest was to work through the Protestant government.' The policy of the British government, in 1969 as now, was clear: to prop up the existing Unionist-dominated state of Northern Ireland at all costs.

Nearly two decades later any talk of British troops 'keeping the peace' in Northern Ireland is a sick joke. Since the troops were sent in approaching 3000 people have died.

Talk of Britain guaranteeing civil rights for the Catholic population is an even sicker joke. In 1985 the British government's own figures showed that in Northern Ireland Catholics were three times more likely to be unemployed than Protestants, suffered greater poverty and poorer housing, schools and social services. The proportion of Catholics on the dole in relation to Protestants has increased every year since the troops went in. As regards discrimination, in 1986 the British government's own Fair

Employment Agency reported cases of discrimination against Catholics by employers as diverse as building societies, the Ulster Museum, the ambulance service and Shorts Engineering. Shorts is Northern Ireland's single biggest employer; just 5 per cent of the workforce there is Catholic. For years the British government was the majority shareholder in Shorts but did nothing to alter this state of affairs. Civil rights have in fact been eroded: between 1975 and 1986, 44,273 people were arrested and held under the Emergency Provisions Act, and 40,933 of these were released without charge.

Again and again British governments have blamed the Northern Ireland troubles on a few 'gangsters' or the 'murderous nature' of the Irish. The plain truth is that the Northern Ireland troubles are a product of British rule. Until the British state gets out of Ireland the bloodshed will go on.

The conquest of Ireland

THE HISTORY OF MODERN IRELAND is the story of capitalism's failure to solve the basic problems of Irish society. That remains true today with the continuance of partition between north and south, but the story begins with the conquest of Ireland by the rulers of Britain nearly four centuries ago.

The purpose of that conquest was to seize the wealth of Ireland for the advantage of the British ruling class. Quite simply Ireland was Britain's first colony. As early as the twelfth century English feudal lords had tried to seize estates on Ireland's eastern seaboard, but, despite the support of the English crown, they never gained more than a foothold. For the next four centuries Irish society developed relatively independently, the Anglo-Irish nobility being integrated into a feudal society which developed out of Ireland's clan system.

All this changed in the sixteenth century when the English state set out to bring all of Ireland under its control. England was now competing with Spain and other states for trade and colonies, and while English merchants cast greedy eyes over Ireland's rich agricultural lands, the English monarchy was nervous that Ireland might fall under Spanish domination. After all, while in England the crown had enforced a new Protestant church, Ireland remained Catholic.

Throughout the sixteenth century the English crown waged a bloody war of conquest in Ireland. By the end of the century it had succeeded in crushing the resistance of the Irish nobility, who held out longest in the historic province of Ulster.

In order to preserve control in Ulster, the new English rulers decided to settle the area with loyal colonists. Whole districts were parcelled off to various lords and to the merchant companies of London—which is why the county of Derry became known as 'Londonderry'. A source of willing settlers was found in the Lowlands of Scotland, settlers all too eager to farm better lands and take advantage of generous leases and low rents.

Previous attempts at such settlement had failed, but the close links between Scotland and Ulster helped ensure the success of this attempt. The native Irish were either driven into the hills or forced to pay rents that were double those paid by the settlers.

The first 'clearance' of Ulster was not fully successful. In 1641 the native Irish rose up. For eight years, while civil war raged between king and parliament in England, control of Ireland was contested between the native Irish, the royalist Anglo-Irish nobility, and supporters of the English parliament who were centred on the cities of Derry and Belfast.

It was Oliver Cromwell, ruler of England after the execution of king Charles I, who set out to reimpose rule from London. Landing in Ireland, he set about crushing the forces of both the royalists and the native Irish chiefs. At the siege of Drogheda his troops massacred the royalist defenders of the town. In an effort to subdue the country he then tried to force the native Irish into Connacht, the poor western province of Ireland. His slogan became 'To Hell or Connacht'.

Forty years later the Irish made another attempt to resist the conquest by allying themselves with James II, who had been deposed as king of Britain by William of Orange in the 'Glorious Revolution'. But William's troops defeated those of James at the Battle of the Boyne in 1690. Ironically the Protestant William was at this time allied with the pope, who celebrated William's victory at the Boyne with a high mass.

Today the struggle in Ireland is often pictured as centring on religion. Why did religion become important in Ireland?

An important effect of the conquest of Ireland was the imposition of the Protestant religion on a country where the mass of the population were Catholics. Along with foreign landlords a foreign church was imposed. The Anglican Church of Ireland became the established state church. Despite the fact that 90 per cent of the population were Catholic each parish was given an Anglican church. The cost of its upkeep and the salaries of its clergy were imposed on the impoverished peasants.

All the old institutions of Irish society were destroyed by the new colonial rulers, but the one body which seemed to remain as a symbol of opposition throughout Ireland was the Catholic church. As the weight of colonial rule worsened, the identification of the mass of the peasantry and the church grew. The same thing is still happening today. In a situation of repression, where workers and peasants reject the ideas by which the ruling administration governs, the Catholic church has become a focus for resistance in Poland and Latin America.

The conquest of Ireland did not centre on religion but on Britain's desire to accumulate profits. But in the process it created religious differences which remain important today. One other thing has to be added. When Irish peasants and workers began to fight back against their oppression, they almost always met with hostility from the Catholic church hierarchy.

By the beginning of the eighteenth century the bulk of Ireland was in the hands of landowners who had been granted land by the British crown or who totally collaborated with the colonial regime. Most were Anglicans—as proof of their loyalty to the crown, which headed the Church of England—and to guarantee their monopoly of power a series of laws was passed barring the remaining native Irish landlords, who remained Catholic, from public office and denying the peasantry basic civil rights.

These penal laws excluded Catholics from voting, sitting in parliament or on the local council, or holding posts within the administration. Other restrictions affected the ownership of land, the right to possess arms and the right to print newspapers. A mere 15 per cent of the land was owned by the native population.

Thus one section of the population, in particular the Protestant landlords, received privileges in return for their loyalty to England. But England's emerging capitalist class were also determined to prevent Ireland developing into an economic rival. If that meant conflict with the Protestant settlers of Ulster, then so be it. When imports of Irish livestock led to a drop in agricultural prices and rents in Britain parliament hurriedly banned imports from Ireland. When the largely Protestant livestock farmers tried exporting elsewhere another law banned that too.

At a time when Britain was entering the industrial revolution, a whole series of import controls were passed banning Irish goods from Britain and its other colonies. By cutting off Ireland's fledgeling industries from these markets, such controls acted as a massive barrier to the development of Ireland's economy. Laws banned Irish companies from processing Irish wool. Instead it had to be sent to Britain. Other laws were passed concerning the Irish cotton trade, the glass trade, sugar refining, brewing and fish curing.

In Dublin there was an Irish parliament but this was made up entirely of Anglican landlords. Any decisions it made had to be approved by the British parliament at Westminster.

All this had the effect of driving the infant Irish capitalist class, who wished to develop industry in Ireland, into opposition to British rule. And this opposition was centred on the Protestant businessmen of Belfast and the surrounding area. In the 1780s and early 1790s cotton mills powered by the latest technology grew up around Belfast. Shipbuilding began too. During the 1780s, when Britain was hard-pressed fighting a war against revolutionary America and its French ally, these industrialists joined with the nobility to win extra powers for the Dublin parliament.

Once the pressure was off, however, Britain began to withdraw these concessions. The nobility, rather than fight, submitted. It was at this point that what we now term republicanism came into existence. Among the manufacturers and artisans of Belfast the idea of securing full Irish independence grew more attractive. Independence would allow Irish industry to develop free from British-imposed restrictions. The British colonies in America had just won their independence, and the ideas of the French revolution too had a powerful effect on the Protestants of Belfast. The execution of the French king Louis XVI was welcomed in Belfast with a fireworks display and open rejoicing.

The revolution had a similar impact throughout Europe. In Germany and Italy, which were divided into a patchwork of little states run on feudal lines by all-powerful monarchs, republican ideas grew. In 1791 the United Irishmen—Ireland's first republican organisation—were formed in Belfast. Its leadership was made up of Protestant radicals. Their aim was an independent republic based on the experience in France.

So modern Irish republicanism was founded by the ancestors

of the Unionist leaders of today's Northern Ireland! And in line with their support for independence and for the 'rights of man'—the new liberty upheld by the French revolution—they were prepared to champion civil rights for Catholics.

Republican ideas were dangerous, not only for Britain's rulers but also for the Irish nobility. The United Irishmen quickly faced repression. Increasingly they began to look to an uprising aided by the French in order to secure an Irish Republic. Deserted by the nobility and most of the middle classes, who were linked to the British administration, the United Irishmen were forced to look to the Irish peasantry for support.

The eighteenth century had seen a tradition of peasant revolt in the Irish countryside. Again and again landlords had tried to drive up rents or evict peasants to make way for livestock, which was more profitable. Again and again the peasants had formed themselves into local bands to exact vengeance on the landlords. Even in Ulster the descendants of the Scottish settlers found their landlords, fellow Protestants, trying to force huge rent increases as their original leases came to an end.

In December 1796 a French fleet anchored off Bantry Bay in the south-west of Ireland. On board was the leader of the United Irishmen, Wolfe Tone. A full-scale rising seemed imminent. But a storm dispersed the fleet and the British authorities immediately began a vicious programme of repression. Troops toured country areas torturing peasants to discover details of their military organisation.

The British ruling class had reason to be scared. Their war with revolutionary France was going badly. In 1797 the London mob stoned the king, crying 'Peace, bread, no war, no king!' That year 50,000 seamen mutinied at Spithead and the Nore, taking over the fleet, electing delegate committees and raising the red flag.

By May 1798 the repression was such that the United Irishmen had to act. French aid no longer seemed possible, but despite that plans were made for a nationwide rising.

It never happened. Repression had beheaded the movement in many areas. In Dublin a rising was betrayed by informers. But in two areas—the counties of Wicklow and Wexford, Down and Antrim—powerful Irish forces took the field. In the latter case the United Irishmen's forces were largely of Protestant radicals. In

Wexford in particular the rising became a rebellion of the oppressed peasantry. It took 30,000 British troops to suppress it.

In isolation the rebellions were brutally crushed. Their leaders were executed. But just as that was happening a small French army landed on the west coast, rallied peasant support, and began a march on Dublin. While they in turn were being defeated a more powerful French fleet, again with Tone on board, was dispersed by the British navy off the northern coast.

The 1798 rising wasn't defeated just by the power of the British state. Ranged against it were Ireland's landlords, big and small, the middle class of the capital, Dublin, and the Catholic church. All were terrified by the revolutionary ideas of the United Irishmen and the threat to property posed by the peasantry. Well might the Protestant leader of the United Irishmen, Henry Joy McCracken of Antrim, write: 'The Rich always betray the Poor.'

Chapter two
Famine, home rule and resistance

THROUGHOUT the nineteenth century resistance to British rule in Ireland continued. There were several attempts by republicans to follow the example of 1798, with unsuccessful risings in 1803, 1848 and 1867. But an important division was emerging.

During the years after the 1798 rising the employers in the Belfast area became integrated into Britain's fast-developing industrial economy. Because of these links, they would turn their backs on any ideas of Irish independence and become the cornerstone of British rule in Ireland.

But for the majority of Ireland British rule meant a block on industrial development, the dominance of absentee landlords who spent the proceeds of Irish rents in London, and the maintenance of a low-level agricultural economy. The bankers, lawyers and native landlords of southern Ireland continued to oppose British colonial rule. They rejected republican ideas of an armed rising, looking instead to constitutional means of changing things, but they remained a thorn in the side of the British ruling class throughout the nineteenth century.

The contrast between the development of the Belfast area and what was happening in the rest of Ireland would be reflected in the development of two different ideologies, Unionism and Nationalism, reflecting the two sections of Ireland's divided ruling class.

Ireland was now under direct rule from London. In 1800 the Dublin parliament had been abolished. By now the massive growth of industry in Britain meant there was little threat of competition from Ireland. All customs barriers were removed. Most of Irish industry, now faced with an influx of cheaper British goods, went into sharp decline.

The main source of livelihood for the mass of people remained the land—which continued to be owned by British or absentee Irish landlords. Ireland exported wheat, other grain and livestock to Britain. After paying the high rents charged by the landlords and tithes to the Anglican Church of Ireland, the peasants were left impoverished. Increasingly they depended for their diet on the potato.

While Britain's imperialist rulers harked on about their 'civilising' role in the world, the truth was that in Ireland the mass of the people saw their standard of living cut to subsistence level. Ireland was a wealthy country, but that wealth went straight to Britain. The Irish Poor Law Commission reported in the 1830s that the total value of Ireland's agricultural production was £36 million. The peasantry received a mere £5 million of this. Of the rest, the landlords took £10 million in rent, while merchants, moneylenders and other middlemen took about £20 million. What was left went to the Church of Ireland in tithes.

At the same time more than half the population were out of work for more than half the year. 'Out of work and in distress during 30 weeks of the year: not less than 585,000 persons, which, with those dependent on them, will make a total of 2,385,000 persons requiring support for 20 weeks in the year,' reported the Commission.

Landlords and their agents enforced ruthless evictions against anyone who got behind with their rent, pulling down their cottages and adding their lands into larger farms. A witness to a House of Commons committee described how in just two parishes more than a thousand people had been evicted, including many old people who 'became beggars and a good many of them died of want'.

During the 1830s the peasantry refused to pay church tithes, which totalled a tenth of their crops. The British army was sent to collect the tithes. Throughout Ireland there were clashes between peasants and British troops. Whole areas were under military occupation.

The result of all this could only be catastrophe. In 1845 the potato crop, on which the peasants depended, failed. The next five years would see further crop failures. The result was famine. More than two million people died. Another million emigrated, starting a pattern that would last generations. At the beginning of the 1840s Ireland's population stood at eight and a half million. By the end of the century it was just five million—and it would continue to fall until the 1960s.

British history portrays the famine as some natural disaster. True, the potato crop failed. But the famine was man-made. There was enough food in Ireland to feed everyone. In 1848, while hundreds of thousands of people died of starvation, nearly two million quarters of grain were exported to Britain. While people starved, the food that could have kept them alive continued to be sold abroad. The landlords and merchants maintained the sacred rights of property and profit, backed by the British government, at awful cost.

Ireland after the famine was a ruined country. Its population was now reduced to little more than cheap labour for the expanding industries of Britain and America. Today Ireland remains one of the poorest countries in Europe—the result of British colonial rule.

The tragedy was that the leaders of Irish nationalism were unable to build a movement capable of preventing this.

The 1840s saw a great class unrest spread across Europe. 1842 saw Britain's first general strike and the rise of the Chartists, who fought for the liberty of British workers and contained a large revolutionary minority. 1848 saw the people of Paris topple the monarchy and trigger a wave of similar uprisings throughout Europe's capitals. In Ireland opposition to British rule centred on the figure of Daniel O'Connell, the 'father of Irish nationalism'.

O'Connell's first campaign had been for the repeal of the penal laws against Catholics. Aided by the Catholic church hierarchy he mobilised rallies that attracted massive support among the peasantry. The British government backed down. But this in no way benefited the majority of Catholics. Britain's limited electoral system gave votes only to the wealthy few, and the impoverished Irish fell well below the necessary property qualification. The changes gave votes to well-off Catholic property owners—and got O'Connell into parliament at Westminster.

After this O'Connell set out to organise a similar campaign to gain home rule. He wanted a Dublin parliament to run Ireland's affairs. It was a modest demand, but brought down the hysteria of the British ruling class on O'Connell's head. Another series of monster rallies showed that O'Connell had mass support among the peasantry and the working class of Dublin. When the final rally outside Dublin was banned by the British, O'Connell tamely called it off. Rather than brave British repression he brought his campaign to an end.

The truth was that O'Connell was himself a landlord. His backers among the Catholic church hierarchy, the landowners and the like opposed British colonial rule but feared a repeat of 1798. In Dublin trade union organisation was spreading—only to be bitterly denounced by O'Connell. On the land peasants withheld their tithes and began meeting rent rises with force. They were hurriedly denounced from the pulpit by the Catholic bishops.

O'Connell looked to constitutional means and saw mass mobilisations as simply a means to pressurise the British administration. He established a political tradition that remains to this day.

But many of the young intellectuals around O'Connell rejected his surrender and began to propagate republican ideas. The Young Ireland group, as they were known, drew on the ideas of European revolutionaries. For this they were denounced by O'Connell and the bishops as anti-Catholic.

As famine spread, the Young Irelanders decided to organise a rising in 1848. But they still hoped to win support from the landlords and the property-owning elite. At a time when the mass of peasants were starving, when the best land was owned by a few landlords, the Young Irelanders refused to demand that land be given to the peasants.

The vicious denunciations by the Catholic bishops and O'Connell's followers gave the green light to the British authorities to suppress the Young Irelanders. An attempt at a rising was badly prepared and failed to mobilise peasant support. The Young Ireland group collapsed.

Again in the 1860s a new republican group, the Fenians, organised strong support. They too were part of a new revolutionary growth across Europe and North America. Many had fought in the American civil war to topple the slave-owning society of the southern states, while others were influenced by socialist ideas from Paris.

In Ireland itself new legislation and the mass emigration that followed the famine allowed a whole class of Irish landlords to buy up land. Again and again they forced up rents and the peasants fought back. In this situation the Fenians gained mass support in the worst-affected areas of the Irish countryside. In turn this meant they were bitterly opposed by the Catholic hierarchy and the emerging capitalist class. In 1863 the pope issued a general condemnation of the Fenians. In 1870 the Bishop of Kerry declared that for them 'eternity is not long enough nor hell hot enough'.

The Fenians, in line with republican ideas popular across Europe, stood for a new form of government in which church and state would be separate. This increased the bishops' hatred for them.

But for all their heroism and daring the Fenians could not translate their widespread support into active opposition that could topple British rule. They still hoped to win support among Irish capitalists and landowners. Despite their radical leanings the Fenians failed to place themselves at the head of the unrest on the land. Instead they hoped to end British rule through secretly organised military action. They first launched an invasion of British-ruled Canada by Irish exiles in the United States. Then a poorly prepared rising in Ireland also failed, as did a bombing campaign in Britain. The repression that followed reduced their popular support—though a Fenian-inspired organisation continued to exist and would win the future leaders of the 1916 rising.

The Fenians had genuine popular support, and this was reflected in the election of Fenian prisoners as members of the Westminster parliament. But in the years that followed it was the resurgence of constitutional nationalism which would organise popular opposition to British rule.

The support for the Fenians had scared sections of the British ruling class into accepting the need for changes in the way they ran Ireland. The Liberal government headed by William Gladstone began to push through reforms. In 1869 they abolished the tithes the peasants had to pay to the Anglican church. Faced with the re-emergence of a constitutional nationalist movement, Gladstone went further and was prepared to grant a degree of home rule to Ireland.

In 1877 a young Protestant lawyer, Charles Parnell, was elected leader of the recently formed Irish Home Rule Party. In order to achieve its goal Parnell adopted radical tactics. In the British parliament he organised the obstruction of business. In Ireland he organised meetings and demonstrations.

More important, he was prepared for a time to back growing unrest on the land. A former Fenian, Michael Davitt, had formed the Land League to oppose rent increases and evictions. The league organised thousands of peasants in opposition to the landlords, the police and British troops—and Parnell agreed to back it. By 1882 civil war seemed near.

Gladstone's government was determined to crush opposition on the land. Davitt was jailed and the British troops fired on peasant demonstrators. Parnell himself was eventually jailed. By then he and his backers had realised that a successful peasant uprising would threaten their own property interests too, and Parnell was ready to enter into a secret pact with Gladstone. In return for promising to uphold British 'law and order' on the land and the repression of the Land League, Parnell was assured that Gladstone would grant limited home rule.

A series of land Acts was now passed that guaranteed loans so that the better-off peasants could buy their land. The remainder who couldn't afford this were transformed into agricultural labourers for this new layer of small farmers, or forced to emigrate. Gladstone, with Parnell's backing, thus solved the land problem by splitting the peasantry along class lines.

In 1885 a general election left Gladstone dependent on Parnell's support in order to have a parliamentary majority. To secure this, Gladstone introduced an Irish Home Rule Bill. On paper the Liberals were committed to the idea. Moreover Gladstone believed that Britain could come to terms with Parnell. But he was out of step with the majority of the British ruling class, including key sections of his own party.

Ireland was economically important to British capitalism. This was the golden age of imperialism. British imperial interests were now competing with German and French rivals. Irish home rule was seen as a blow to the empire. In order to block it the Tories made common cause with the industrialists in Belfast. Sir Randolph Churchill, father of the future Sir Winston, visited Belfast, warning that 'Ulster will fight and Ulster will be right'. He was openly threatening armed rebellion backed by the Tories against an elected British government. Privately he wrote:

I decided some time ago that if [Gladstone] went for home rule, the Orange card would be the one to play. Please God it may turn out the ace of trumps and not the two.

In the event the Liberals split and Gladstone's Home Rule Bill was defeated. Parnell himself was forced by the Catholic hierarchy to resign as party leader after he became involved in a divorce case.

In many ways this had been the best opportunity for Ireland to gain a degree of independence through constitutional means. Countries such as Italy and Germany had achieved national unity and independence in this period, but for Ireland this path was blocked by the interests of British imperialism.

The direct legacy of British rule in the nineteenth century was an Ireland split between two distinct economies. In Belfast there was now one of the most up-to-date industrial economies in the world by the standards of the time. Elsewhere living standards and economic standards had actually fallen. And the price of British rule was all too evident in the millions of deaths from starvation, the millions who were forced to leave Ireland in order to survive, and the continuing rural poverty of western Ireland.

Chapter three

Marx, Engels and the Irish Question

IN JANUARY 1848—that year of European revolution—Friedrich Engels greeted the news that the Chartists, Britain's first mass working-class movement, were campaigning for Irish freedom:

> There can be no doubt that henceforth the mass of the Irish people will unite more closely with the English Chartists and will act with them according to a common plan. As a result the victory of the English democrats and hence the liberation of Ireland will be hastened by many years.

Before the defeat of Chartism both Karl Marx and Friedrich Engels, who were to be life-long collaborators, were convinced that the liberation of Ireland would follow from the success of British workers. After the Chartists' revolutionary challenge to the British state collapsed, Marx spent much of the 1850s and 1860s examining how Ireland had been subjugated by England, how British policies were the cause of the great famine, how British landlords were evicting hundreds of thousands of Irish peasants and replacing them with cattle, and how this was supplying the industrial cities of Britain and America with cheap labour. Marx's book **Capital** contains a powerful critique of British rule in Ireland.

With the rise of the Fenian movement, the Irish question again became an important issue for British workers. The level of the movement in Ireland was now higher than it was in Britain, where the class struggle was reviving only slowly.

Marx was clear that the Fenians were not a working-class movement, though they had 'socialistic tendencies'. He dismissed any notion that the Fenians could usher in socialism. Nevertheless he held that an essentially peasant movement could break the power of the Anglo-Irish ascendancy, achieving both an agrarian revolution and Irish independence.

Marx and Engels threw themselves into winning support for the Fenians and in particular for republican prisoners in British jails. Marx himself played a central role in organising a mass demonstration in 1869 demanding the release of Fenian prisoners. Their main concern, however, was to bring about the revolution in Britain itself, writing that:

> To hasten the social revolution in England is the most important object of the International Working Men's Association. The sole means of hastening it is to make Ireland independent.

Marx insisted that British workers had to support Irish independence:

> I have become more and more convinced—and the only question is to drive this conviction home to the English working class—that it can never do anything decisive here in England until it separates its policy with regard to Ireland most definitely from the policy of the ruling classes, until it not only makes common cause with the Irish, but actually takes the initiative in dissolving the Union [of Britain and Ireland] established in 1801 and replacing it by a free federal relationship. And this must be done not as a matter of sympathy with Ireland but as a demand made in the interests of the English proletariat.

Thus Marx pronounced that: 'Any nation that oppresses another forges its own chains.'

Marx wrote of the British revolution that 'the lever must be applied in Ireland'. He had two reasons for believing this. The first reason is of less interest today: he regarded income from Irish rents as the bulwark of the English aristocracy. Irish independence and the consequent expropriation of their estates would, he argued, bring down the ruling class in Britain. This analysis was simply wrong. By the late nineteenth century the British landowning class was in a steep economic and political decline. The diminishing importance of Irish rents for the maintenance of the British ruling class was demonstrated by Gladstone's ability to transfer most of the Anglo-Irish estates to the Catholic peasantry.

More interesting was Marx's second argument for supporting Irish liberation. The oppression of Ireland, he said, helped to cement British workers to their own ruling class:

> Every industrial and commercial centre in England now possesses a working class *divided* into two *hostile* camps, English proletarians and Irish proletarians. The ordinary English worker hates the Irish worker as a competitor who lowers his standard of life. In relation to the Irish worker he feels himself a member of the *ruling* nation and so turns himself into a tool of the aristocrats and capitalists *against Ireland*, thus strengthening their domination *over himself*. He cherishes religious, social and national prejudices against the Irish worker. His attitude towards him is much the same as that of the 'poor whites' to the 'niggers' in the former slave states of the USA... This *antagonism* is the *secret of the impotence of the English working class*...

In the middle decades of the nineteenth century Irish immigrant workers formed a large percentage of the working class in Britain's industrial centres, roughly proportional to the size of the black working class in the northern cities of the USA today. Describing the Manchester of 1844, Engels wrote:

> The rapid extension of English industry could not have taken place if England had not possessed in the numerous and impoverished population a reserve to command. The Irish had nothing to lose at home, and much to gain in England... These Irishmen... migrate for fourpence to England, on the deck of a steamship in which they are often packed like cattle... The worst dwellings are good enough for them; their clothing causes them little trouble... shoes they know not; their food consists of potatoes and potatoes only; whatever they earn beyond their need they spend on drink. What does such a race want with high wages?

Irish peasants, forced off the land, migrated to England and Scotland, competing for work and often undermining wages and working conditions. In the 1850s and 1860s, after the defeat of Chartism, anti-Irish ideas spread, and this was often reflected in the growth of the Orange Lodge in areas such as Clydeside, Liverpool, Tyneside and the cotton towns of Lancashire.

But there was still another tradition among British workers. Irishmen such as Feargus O'Connor and Bronterre O'Brien had been among the leaders of Chartism, and support for Ireland's fight against British rule had been a central part of the Chartist agitation. Again in the 1860s and 1870s the demand for amnesty for Fenian prisoners won widespread support among British workers. The demonstration of November 1887 which came to be known as 'Bloody Sunday', when armed soldiers and police attacked the demonstrators, was called to oppose repression in Ireland. The division between Irish and British workers largely disappeared at the end of the century with the experience of common struggle around the New Unions of the 1890s and the Great Unrest just before the First World War.

Marx's clear support for the Fenians against British colonialism was not, however, uncritical. In 1868 there was a mass torchlight meeting outside Clerkenwell jail in London, in support of the 'Manchester Martyrs', three Fenians who faced public execution for attempting to rescue an arrested comrade. A few days later the Fenians set off a bomb outside the jail in an attempt to rescue them, destroying a working-class tenement and killing twelve people. Marx did not spare his words, describing the bombing as 'melodramatic folly' and arguing that it would harm the Fenians' support: 'English workers could hardly be expected to regard being blown up by Fenian emissaries as an honour.'

The real importance of the Irish question for Marx was that, in order to win British workers to socialism and to create genuine unity with the Irish migrants who worked alongside them, the British labour movement had to champion Irish freedom.

Later Lenin would extend this argument, insisting that workers in the imperialist countries of the world must support the right of oppressed nations to self-determination. Not only would this help break the links which bound the workers of the imperialist countries to their ruling classes, but such liberation struggles would also weaken world capitalism and aid the international struggle of workers.

For both Marx and Lenin, the starting point for support for national liberation was not some abstract principle or moral criterion—but what best served the interests of the working class in its fight for international socialism. Above all, the advice that Marx and Engels gave to British workers was not to waste time over pious expressions of sympathy. Recognise that your own enemy and that of the Irish people is the British ruling class. Defeat your own enemies at home and you will have struck a decisive blow for the social liberation of all oppressed countries.

Chapter four
The roots of sectarianism

THE THREAT OF HOME RULE in the late nineteenth century had been met by a powerful mobilisation in the north-east corner of Ireland, centred on Belfast. An alliance emerged there linking Protestant workers and their bosses, an alliance based on sectarianism against the Catholic population.

Sectarianism in rural northern Ireland was nothing new. During the 1790s there had been clashes between Catholic peasants and Protestant landowners in County Armagh. To defend their interests the landowners had organised themselves into the Orange Lodge—which was open only to Protestants. The British government encouraged and armed the lodge, using it to help suppress the 1798 uprising—when its members were used against the mainly Protestant forces of the United Irishmen.

For the first half of the nineteenth century the Orange Lodge remained relatively small, being based on yeomen farmers in rural areas of northern Ireland. In towns the political tradition, while no longer republican, remained liberal and non-sectarian.

The industrial development of the Belfast area changed all this. The one section of Irish industry to prosper was the textile industry of the north-east. During the Napoleonic wars new orders flooded in. Then, though the cotton industry was destroyed in an economic slump during the 1820s, a new linen industry arose based on factory production. Shipbuilding too began to expand.

These industries looked to Britain. Scots banks supplied capital. Scots mines supplied coal. British industrialists supplied expertise (climaxing with Harland the shipbuilder). The British Empire guaranteed markets. Even before the famine the rest of Ireland could not compete with such a pull. As the Irish socialist

James Connolly wrote a hundred years later:

> ...tell me how poor Ireland, exhausted and drained of her lifeblood at every pore, with a population almost wholly agricultural and unused to mechanical pursuits, is to establish new factories, and where is she to find customers to get them going?

Belfast's employing class was tied to Britain's empire, but other developments on the British pattern terrified them. The early decades of the nineteenth century were years of mass unrest among the new working class in Britain, unrest that spread to Antrim, Down and Belfast. One historian of local industry has written:

> As early as 1802 the **Belfast Newsletter** was concerned about the extent of trade unionism in the town. In 1811, a great cotton operatives' union for the whole of the United Kingdom was in existence. Not only were the weavers of Belfast organised, but those in the country around Lisburn as well. In April 1815, a large number of workers from the Maze marched into Belfast and left their webs unwoven as a protest against reduced wages. When the magistrates attempted to arrest the leaders rioting broke out.
>
> (E R R Green, **The Lagan Valley**)

In both 1816 and 1817 there were further uprisings by the weavers of Belfast and Lisburn. The following year there was another big strike. But the struggle ended in victory for the employers and cuts in wages, for the decline of the cotton industry destroyed the weavers' organisation. It was in the wake of this defeat and in the growing competition for jobs in the new linen mills that sectarianism found roots.

Belfast itself grew from a population of 28,000 in 1813 to 100,300 in 1851. The new industries began to suck in cheap labour from the surrounding areas. In 1812 Catholics made up a mere seventh of Belfast's population; by 1834 two-fifths were Catholics. Most were from impoverished rural areas. They found themselves competing for jobs with Protestants from similar areas. Desperate for work, they were cheap labour, often cheaper than Belfast's own Protestant workers, and the competition for jobs was most severe among the unskilled and lowest paid.

1835 saw Belfast's first sectarian riot. A pattern was beginning to develop. The famine and further Catholic migration to the towns in search of jobs saw the Orange Lodge begin to grow in Belfast. Before then it had had little or no presence. By 1857 there were 35 lodges in the city with 1333 members, and by 1870 more than 100 lodges with 4000 members.

Their membership came largely from the poorer, unskilled Protestant workers. Sectarian violence in particular centred on the poorest Protestant areas, Sandy Row and the Shankill Road, which were alongside Catholic working-class ghettos.

This change paralleled what was happening to the political outlook of Belfast's industrialists. Home rule would spell disaster for their industries, based as they were on integration with Britain. The rural unrest also terrified them. Politically their interests were counterposed to those of the nationalist middle class to the south. Increasingly they began to look to the maintenance of sectarianism as a bulwark against home rule. The British authorities helped show the way by arming Orangemen at the time of the 1848 republican uprising. Sectarianism also offered clear benefits day-to-day, as it kept workers divided and so helped guarantee profits.

Gladstone's Home Rule Bills of the 1880s saw former Liberal industrialists rushing to join the Orange Lodges. One former Liberal MP announced that 'the Orange Society is alone capable of dealing with the conditions of anarchy and rebellion which prevail in Ireland'. The spread of the Land League to Protestant farmers added to the alarm.

What opposition was there to sectarianism? The republicans were of course non-sectarian but during the 1880s and 1890s they were a tiny minority. The Home Rule Party seemed dominated by the Catholic bishops, and their dismissal of Parnell served only to flame Orange propaganda about 'Rome Rule'.

There was of course the trade union movement. The 1870s had seen strikes in the shipyards. Belfast had strong unions but these were to be found mainly among highly skilled workers. As in Britain, the skilled made no attempt to organise the vast bulk of the unskilled—whether Protestant or Catholic. Such a narrow sectional view meant they weren't prepared to raise wider questions. When confronted with sectarianism they simply went along with it.

The threat of home rule consolidated the Unionist alliance of Protestant boss and worker that we now see celebrated each year on the anniversary of the Battle of the Boyne. The alliance was cemented too by firms such as Mackies and Short Brothers Engineering, which ensured that they took on only Protestant workers. The Orange Lodge became the means of finding work.

Protestant workers came to enjoy certain privileges. For instance in the docks Protestant workers were employed on cross-channel traffic, which offered regular employment; Catholics worked the deep-sea docks, which offered only casual work.

In the shipyards and engineering plants of Belfast, which were almost exclusively Protestant, skilled workers enjoyed better pay than their colleagues on the Tyne and the Clyde. But the majority of Protestant workers were unskilled labourers whose wage packets were much smaller than those of their British counterparts. For rural labourers in Protestant areas such as Down and Antrim wages were nearly half those in Britain.

For women workers in the textile mills things were even worse. An unskilled carder at the beginning of this century had a life expectancy of less than 17 years. Union organisation among the unskilled was virtually nil and this was reflected in poor safety conditions for Protestant and Catholic workers alike. Protestant labourers and their families lived in slums little better than their Catholic counterparts.

But in this situation even marginal privileges were prized. If the Orange Lodge controlled access to key jobs then that cemented support for its sectarian stance. Protestant workers might suffer, but like the poor whites of the southern states of America who looked down on the blacks, they could look down on the Catholics who were worse off than themselves. In Eamonn McCann's words, it remains a case of 'tuppence ha'penny looking down on tuppence'.

Capitalism created sectarianism. At root it was based on the way Irish capitalism developed. While most of Ireland was forced into a backward agricultural economy, in Belfast there grew up industries that in their time were among the most advanced in the world. This development created the material base for sectarianism, and eventually for partition.

Chapter five
'The divine gospel of discontent'

'THE IRISH WORKING CLASS must emancipate itself, and in emancipating itself it must, perforce, free its own country.'

So wrote James Connolly, the great Irish socialist, in 1897. At that time Connolly was organiser of the Irish Socialist Republican Party—Ireland's first socialist organisation. The IRSP did not survive long, and its failure forced Connolly to emigrate to America, where he stayed until 1910. By the time of his return the Irish working class had entered Irish politics centre-stage.

In 1907 James Larkin had arrived in Belfast as an official of the British-based dockers' union. On his arrival he announced his intention to preach 'a divine gospel of discontent'. Larkin had been born in Liverpool of Irish parents. He was a socialist and a firm supporter of Irish independence. Two years earlier he'd been fired from his job in the Liverpool docks.

In the Belfast docks only 1000 of the 3000 dockers held permanent jobs. The rest were employed casually. The dockers worked long hours in all weathers. Their pay was a miserly tuppence per ton of material moved. They were lucky if they got a full week's work. Within three months of Larkin's arrival 2900 dockers were in the union; he had also organised the 1500 carters who worked in the docks.

The employers responded by locking out union members. It was a full-scale attempt to break union organisation. Larkin responded by bringing out all the dockers on strike, and then the carters.

The strikers were denounced by Unionist politicians, the Catholic church and pro-home rule bosses alike. British troops occupied Belfast docks while strike-breaking labour was brought in from Britain and southern Ireland. But the strike grew in strength. The Independent Orange Order, originally a right-wing breakaway from the Orange Lodge, swung over to provide solid support for the strikers. On 12 July collections for the strikers were held on both Orange walks. The visiting Scottish revolutionary John Maclean described the atmosphere:

> Workers have gone mad on trade unionism, and are rushing up to all the prominent men in the strike, wanting to join a union—any union... They are rolling up in tens of thousands to the Custom House steps on Sundays to listen to the revolutionary gospel of socialism.

More than 100,000 workers marched down the Protestant Shankill Road in a march involving both Orange and nationalist flute bands. Then, to the terror of the bosses, more than half the Belfast police force—the forerunners of today's RUC—mutinied after Larkin had drawn attention to their poor pay and conditions.

The mutiny was suppressed, but the Unionist establishment failed in a planned attempt to break the strike by triggering sectarian violence. Some 3000 British troops invaded the Catholic Falls Road. Crowds were charged by cavalry and by troops with bayonets. Two innocent workers were killed when troops opened fire. The Unionist press pictured this as a 'nationalist insurrection', warning of attacks on Protestant areas. But Larkin and the strike leaders prevented any division among the strikers by stressing their unity as members of the working class.

The strike was broken not by sectarianism but by the intervention of the head of the dockers' union Larkin represented. James Sexton, terrified by the unrest in Belfast, crossed from England to reach an unfavourable agreement with the bosses over the heads of the strikers. The euphoria of the strike was quickly replaced by bitter demoralisation.

Despite its defeat, the strike had made a great advance in building the solidarity and unity of the Belfast workers. The tragedy was that despite the growth in militancy there was no socialist organisation in Belfast which could maintain this.

The Independent Labour Party, to which Larkin himself belonged, had a policy of trying to build electoral support by stressing common social issues—but it did not take a position on Irish independence, believing this to be 'divisive'. In the search for votes this meant in practice bowing down before the predominant views of the largely Protestant working class.

The leading representative of the party, William Walker, opposed Irish home rule, denounced Catholicism and stressed the 'democratic' tradition of Protestantism in northern Ireland. In a 1905 by-election Walker described himself as 'Unionist in politics'. He answered a questionnaire issued to candidates by an ultra-right wing Unionist group by announcing: 'Protestantism means protesting against superstition and hence true Protestantism is synonymous with Labour.'

Walker was not the only sectarian influence. When Larkin later led a breakaway union in the docks, Sexton used Protestant sectarianism to ensure that the split took place on religious lines. The bosses followed up with an offensive against any trade unionist. In 1912, during the home-rule crisis, some 2400 Catholics and 600 'rotten Prods', many of them union activists, were driven from their jobs in the docks and shipyards. Reaction fed on demoralisation and defeat together with the absence of any socialist opposition to sectarianism.

By now the great unrest sweeping Irish labour was affecting Dublin to the south. At the turn of the century 60 per cent of Dublin's population were working-class. Though not predominantly an industrial city, Dublin was a trading centre and transport work provided the vast majority of jobs. The bulk of workers were either unskilled or employed casually.

Trade unions had been established in Dublin, Belfast and Cork during the 1870s and 1880s but these unions were mainly of the skilled trades. The unskilled labourers suffered low wages and terrible conditions. They might work up to 70 hours a week. In Dublin a third of the population lived in single-room flats in ageing tenements. Dublin's slums were compared to those of Calcutta. More than 30,000 people were evicted each year. Between 1905 and 1912 food prices went up by 25 per cent. Unemployment stood at around 20 per cent.

The 1907 strike led by Larkin opened up a period of labour militancy that shook Ireland from one end to the other. In 1908 Larkin led strikes of Dublin carters and Cork dockers. In 1910 he formed the Irish Transport and General Workers Union. At its start it had 3000 members. Within three years it had 13,000.

Under Larkin's leadership the ITGWU championed the

independence of Ireland. Connolly returned from America to become its Belfast organiser. In 1911 the union produced a paper, the **Irish Worker**. In June it sold 26,000 copies; in July 64,000 copies; in August 74,750 and in September 94,994 copies. The paper pulled no punches, naming names and listing the crimes of the employers and slum landlords.

This development reflected what was happening in Britain. From 1911 until the outbreak of the First World War in 1914 a succession of strikes swept the country. Militants organised workers into general unions which included unskilled workers who had previously been unorganised. The ITGWU was part of this movement.

But the rise of Irish labour coincided with the re-emergence of the whole question of British colonial control. In 1910 a Liberal government was elected which once again relied on MPs of the Irish Home Rule Party for its majority. To secure their support it was forced again to promise home rule.

Among the growing middle class of Dublin and elsewhere in the south there had been a revival of interest in Irish culture and language. Republican ideas again began to draw support among a minority. A Dublin intellectual, Arthur Griffith, founded Sinn Fein—the words, in Gaelic, mean 'Ourselves alone'. This party stood for a dual monarchy under which an Irish parliament would be set up with powers to introduce import controls in order to protect Irish industries and help them grow. Griffith accepted that Ireland would still be under the British crown—and even hoped for a share in administering its empire.

In 1911 Irish home rule seemed inevitable. The Liberal government, dependent on the votes of Irish MPs, had overcome the veto put on a new Bill by the House of Lords. But the problem of northern Ireland remained. The gap between north and south had widened. The area around Belfast now contained nearly half of Ireland's industrial workforce.

As home rule came nearer, Belfast's Unionist bosses prepared to resist. To represent them they selected a former Tory attorney-general, Sir Edward Carson. In Britain the Tory Party and sections of the establishment joined with Carson. This alliance began to threaten civil war if home rule was implemented. In front of 50,000 Orangemen, Carson declared that he was prepared to seize power in Ulster.

In 1912 a covenant was signed by 218,000 people pledging themselves to use 'all means necessary to defeat home rule'. Factory owners led their workforces in signing their names *en masse*. The Tory leader Bonar Law told a monster rally in England: 'I can imagine no length of resistance to which Ulster can go in which I should not be prepared to support them.'

Just as Randolph Churchill had threatened in the 1880s to 'play the Orange card', the Tories were again threatening armed rebellion against an elected British government. These champions of British democracy were quick to drop such notions of democracy when their interests were threatened.

It looked as if civil war between supporters of home rule and the Unionists was imminent.

But in 1913 a new division emerged in Irish society. Dublin was divided by open class war on its streets. The different factions of Ireland's capitalist class hastily buried their differences to join with the British state in defeating the power of the working class.

Ireland's employers had decided to break the new ITGWU at all costs. Lock-outs in Cork and Waterford led up to the decisive confrontation—the great Dublin lock-out of 1913. The city's employers organised themselves into a powerful federation that brought together 400 firms. At its head was William Martin Murphy—the richest man in Dublin, owner of the city's trams and the pro-home rule **Irish Independent**.

In August Murphy locked out all the tramworkers, saying they would be taken back only if they left the ITGWU. The lock-out spread to the **Independent** and Jacob's biscuit factory, also owned by Murphy. Workers throughout the city retaliated by blacking Murphy's goods. Newsboys struck, attacking the strike-breakers taken on to sell the **Independent**. By September 25,000 workers were on strike or locked-out.

On one side stood the working class of Dublin. Round them they rallied republicans such as Padraic Pearse, later to be the key republican figure in the 1916 rising, and intellectuals such as the poet W B Yeats and Countess Markievicz, the 'Red Countess', a daughter of the Anglo-Irish establishment who became a staunch republican.

Facing them were the police, the Unionist establishment, the Catholic hierarchy and even the Home Rule Party—to which Murphy belonged. This clearly saw the strike as a threat to the interests of the section of the Irish capitalist class that it represented. Arthur Griffith of Sinn Fein also waded in, bitterly denouncing Larkin. He believed the strike divided Irish nationalists and urged unity with the likes of Murphy.

The lock-out gave a glimpse of the fundamental division in Irish society—that between the working class and the capitalist class. The likes of Arthur Griffith would later side with the republicans in fighting British rule because it blocked Ireland's capitalist development. But in 1913, when he felt the Irish working class were threatening those same capitalist interests, he was prepared to side with his Unionist opponents. Again nine years later, he and others like him would turn against those republicans they felt were carrying the struggle with Britain too far.

Meanwhile the Dublin lock-out was becoming a crucial test of strength. The day after the tramworkers were locked out Larkin was charged with sedition. He kept up huge meetings in the centre of Dublin. His meetings were banned. Holding up the proclamation to 10,000 workers, Larkin announced: 'I am going to burn the Proclamation of the King... People make kings and people can unmake them.'

The next Sunday police cordoned off the city centre to stop Larkin speaking. Disguised as an old man, he reached the balcony of a big hotel. As he began to speak the police baton-charged. Two workers were killed, 100 arrested and 400 injured. Larkin was jailed.

In response the strikers formed a defence force—the Irish Citizens Army. Clashes continued between police and strikers. The lock-out extended to agricultural labourers. Tension worsened when a slum tenement block collapsed, killing seven people.

Increasingly Larkin and Connolly looked to British trade unions for the blacking needed to defeat the bosses. The strikers and their families suffered greatly. Food ships arrived from Britain. Altogether £150,000 was raised for the strikers—a huge sum in those days—mostly by rank-and-file trade unionists in Britain. British workers organised to take in the children of strikers in order to feed them. But Catholic priests in Dublin whipped up a hysterical mob with allegations that the children would be educated as Protestants. The mob, with priests to the fore, physically attacked the children and their mothers, preventing them from boarding ships that were to take them to Britain.

Larkin and Connolly appealed for solidarity action by British workers. But when several thousand railway workers in England came out in support of the Dublin strikers they were ordered back by their union. In December the British Trades Union Congress met to discuss requests for solidarity action. They rejected further support for the locked-out workers. The attack was led by the former left-winger Ben Tillet, who denounced Larkin. The union officials who dominated the congress were not prepared to back open confrontation with the employers and their state.

Although the lock-out dragged on for another month Larkin and Connolly had to admit defeat. With the end of resistance, the employers launched an all-out offensive, slashing wages. Union membership slumped. Larkin left for America to raise funds, leaving Connolly in charge of the ITGWU.

The tragedy of the Great Dublin Lock-out was that, despite the great militancy, there was no attempt to build a socialist party grouping the best militants. Connolly was an outstanding socialist, but he believed that socialism could be achieved by creating a strong union grouping all workers, aided by a Labour Party which would spread socialist propaganda. The one organisation which did group militants together was the Irish Citizens Army. This remained after the lock-out as a military body, with reduced membership.

But the lock-out had shown how 'champions' of the Irish people such as Murphy, Griffith and the leaders of the Home Rule Party envisaged their 'free' Ireland. With such leaders, even if they could gain a degree of independence from Britain, Connolly warned, Ireland's workers would gain nothing. As he had written earlier:

> If you remove the English army tomorrow and hoist the green flag over Dublin Castle, unless you set about the organisation of the Socialist Republic, your efforts would be in vain.

Chapter six

Easter Week
and the fight for independence

IRELAND HAD GLIMPSED the power that could have achieved real freedom, but now the defeat of the Dublin working class seemed to open the floodgates of reaction. Sectarian violence again flared in Belfast. The Unionist alliance of industrialist, landowner and worker on which the Northern Ireland state would be built was being formed.

What opposition was there to this?

A virtual general strike in Belfast in 1907 and a further rash of strikes in 1911 in which Connolly was involved had been defeated. In their wake the employers had gone on the offensive, destroying union organisation particularly among the unskilled, where Orangeism now blossomed again. The defeat following the Dublin lock-out further weakened the power of the trade unions.

As we shall see, Connolly found himself in a minority among Belfast socialists, who by and large opposed home rule and were prepared to conceal any opposition to sectarianism in order to win wider support. The chief political representative of Belfast's Catholics was Joe Devlin, leader of the city's Home Rule Party. Devlin represented the Catholic middle classes, ran his party as a personal machine and followed policies laid down by the Catholic church. Far from challenging sectarianism, he attempted to form a rival to the Orange Lodge—the Hibernian Order—which itself became involved in sectarian violence.

Connolly found his street meetings attacked by Orange thugs in Protestant areas and by Devlin's thugs in Catholic ones. Devlin and his Home Rule Party seemed to mirror the image painted by Carson, who portrayed supporters of Irish independence as Catholic bigots.

While the Home Rule Bill was being debated by the House of Commons at Westminster, the Unionists set up a 100,000-strong private army, the Ulster Volunteer Force (UVF). A British lieutenant-general was appointed its commanding officer. Tory politicians in Britain raised funds for arms. Then in mid-1913 Carson visited Germany to secure arms supplies from Britain's main imperialist rival.

In November the Irish Volunteers were formed in Dublin to defend home rule. Republicans were heavily involved in their formation. Within a year they had 180,000 members.

In the months leading up to the First World War the British ruling class was deeply split over the question of home rule. The Tories and, it became clear, the officer corps of the army were prepared to go beyond mere rhetoric in opposing it.

In April 1914, despite a ban on arms shipments to Ireland and a naval blockade, the UVF landed 35,000 rifles at Larne. The army and police looked on as the UVF seized the port and sent out armed columns across the country. A month earlier the Liberal government had ordered troops based at the Curragh Camp outside Dublin to move north. Their commanding officer and senior officers refused, after consultation with senior officers in London. After three days the Liberals gave in, announcing that British troops would not be used in Ulster.

After consultation with the War Office the commander of the mutineers, Brigadier-General Hubert Gough, issued a statement with their agreement: 'I got a signed guarantee that in no circumstances shall we be used to force Home Rule on the Ulster people; if it came to civil war, I would fight for Ulster rather than against her.' No wonder the **Morning Post** declared: 'The army has killed the Home Rule Bill.'

The Curragh Mutiny showed that the idea that the army is 'above politics' is pure fiction. Not only that. The British army was also clear which side it was on. In July British troops in Dublin tried to seize arms landed for the Irish Volunteers. Having failed, they met jeering crowds. The troops opened fire, killing three people.

Civil war, possibly spreading to Britain, seemed to threaten. But the Unionists' campaign had convinced the supporters of home rule that even the creation of one Irish parliament under the British crown was impossible. The businessmen and landowners who led both the Unionists and the Home Rule Party reached an agreement in July 1914. Ireland would be partitioned, setting aside the six north-eastern counties—the area that contained the greatest concentration of industry and in which there was a Unionist majority.

Partition reflected the different interests of the two sections of Ireland's capitalist class. The Unionists wanted to retain the integration into the British economy on which their shipyards, textile factories and engineering plants depended. The bosses who backed home rule wished to develop Irish industry separately, by creating import controls in order to keep out cheap British goods. This required the loosening of British economic control. Both sections had been terrified by the labour unrest of recent years. There was no guarantee that Ireland's bosses could maintain control over their workers if conflict grew round the question of home rule. Partition, however, would allow each section of Ireland's bosses to retain their wealth and their control. Further, it would deepen divisions among Ireland's workers.

A month after partition was agreed, the First World War broke out in Europe. Home rule was put on ice. Both the Unionists and the Home Rule Party supported the war. While the UVF volunteered for service in the British army *en masse*, the leader of the Home Rule Party called on the Irish Volunteers too to volunteer for slaughter in the trenches.

Connolly could see that partition and such support for the war was disastrous. Partition would secure the rule of his class opponents, both north and south. Connolly had believed that the European socialist parties would oppose the war. They didn't, instead supporting their own ruling classes. In Dublin thousands of workers flocked to join up, partly because of unemployment in the wake of the lock-out.

Connolly increasingly believed that socialists would have to act against the threat of partition and the growing slaughter. As chief of the Irish Citizens Army, which organised a few hundred Dublin workers, he prepared for a rising against British rule. Meanwhile the republicans had organised a split from the Irish Volunteers which grouped a few thousand people ready to fight for independence. It was these forces which came together to launch the Easter Rising of 1916, an alliance between Connolly's Citizens Army and the republicans led by the poet and teacher

Padraic Pearse and the former Fenian Tom Clarke. Opposed to partition, these middle-class radicals had sympathised with the workers locked-out in 1913.

Yet despite his alliance with the republicans Connolly didn't drop his class politics. Right up to the rising he was involved in socialist and union organisation, leading a strike in Dublin docks. 'In the event of victory,' he told the Citizens Army, 'hold on to your rifles, as those with whom we're fighting may stop before our goal is reached. We are fighting for economic as well as political liberty.' Connolly had just days earlier written in **Workers Republic**:

> We are out for Ireland for the Irish. But who are the Irish? Not the rack-renting, slum-owning landlord; not the sweating, profit-grinding capitalist; not the sleek and oily lawyer; nor the prostitute pressman—the hired liars of the enemy... but the Irish working class...

On Easter Monday 1916 a thousand or so Volunteers, together with a few hundred men and women from the Citizens Army, took over the centre of Dublin. Hopes for a national rising had been destroyed after the Volunteers' commander refused to back a rising at the last moment. Hoped-for German aid was intercepted by the British navy.

In his defence of the Easter Rising, Lenin rejected the view that it was a *putsch*, a military adventure. Defending the rising from left-wing critics, he wrote in 1916:

> Whoever calls *such* an uprising a *'putsch'* is either a hardened reactionary, or a doctrinaire hopelessly incapable of picturing a social revolution as a living thing.
>
> For to imagine that social revolution *is conceivable* without revolts by small nations in the colonies and in Europe, without the revolutionary outbursts of a section of the petty bourgeoisie *with all its prejudices*, without a movement of politically non-conscious proletarian and semi-proletarian masses against landlord, church, monarchial, national and other oppressor—to imagine that means *repudiating social revolution*. Very likely one army will line up in one place and say 'We are for socialism', while another will do so in another place and say 'We are for imperialism', and that will be the

social revolution! Only from such a ridiculously pedantic angle could one label the Irish rebellion a *'putsch'*.

Nevertheless from a socialist view the rising can be criticised. After Connolly entered the alliance with the republicans he accepted their conspiratorial approach, which meant that only a few people knew of the plans for a rising. Only a minority of the republican-led Volunteers took part. Within the Citizens Army there was no serious political debate or planning about what would happen, beyond the initial step of seizing central Dublin.

For a week the rebels held out heroically despite a massive British artillery bombardment which set fire to the city centre. The rising was condemned by the Catholic hierarchy, the leadership of the Home Rule Party and Arthur Griffith of Sinn Fein. Isolated in Dublin and heavily outnumbered, the rebels were forced to surrender. Day after day in the month that followed, the leaders of the rising were executed. Connolly was the last to be shot. Paralysed by a wound, he had to be tied to a chair since he was unable to stand.

Earlier the **Irish Independent**, owned by his opponent in the lock-out, Murphy, had carried a front-page picture of Connolly with the heading 'Let the worst of the ringleaders be singled out and dealt with as they deserve'. Arthur Henderson of the British Labour Party was a member of the cabinet which approved Connolly's execution.

Connolly had hoped that not only would the rising break British rule but it would 'set the torch to a European conflagration that will not burn out till the last throne and the last capitalist bond and debenture will be shrivelled in the funeral pyre of the last war lord'. But beyond urging the members of the Citizens Army to 'hold on to your rifles', he had offered no programme for how the rising might ensure that the working class took the lead in the fight for Irish independence. As Lenin said, the misfortune was 'that they have risen prematurely, when the European revolt of the working class has not yet matured'.

Within two years that would change. Starting in Russia, a revolutionary wave would sweep Europe, affecting Ireland deeply.

Chapter seven

James Connolly
—international socialist

TODAY a variety of political parties in Ireland claim to stand in the tradition of James Connolly. The Irish Labour Party claims his inheritance even while in a coalition with the right-wing Fine Gael party. The Provisionals quote Connolly's writings. Even Eamonn de Valera, founder of Ireland's main capitalist party, Fianna Fail, claimed that he shared the same ideals as Connolly.

But what did Connolly stand for?

Connolly arrived in Ireland in 1896 from Scotland, where he had been born of Irish parents and had become a socialist activist. He had two objectives: to build an independent working-class party where none existed and to bring together the struggle for socialism and the struggle for Irish freedom. Within weeks of arriving he had launched the Irish Socialist Republican Party, whose programme declared: 'The national and economic freedom of the Irish people must be sought in the same direction, *viz* the establishment of an Irish Socialist Republic.'

As we have seen, Connolly argued that only the working class could achieve the national liberation of Ireland as part of its fight for socialism. The Irish capitalist class was incapable of achieving liberation, tied as it was to the international capitalist set-up and fearful of jeopardising its own economic interests by breaking fully with British imperialism.

In advanced countries problems such as national independence or colonial rule were solved by revolutions led by the young capitalist class—this had happened in Britain in the seventeenth century and in America and France at the end of the eighteenth. But Connolly argued that in Ireland this task fell on the shoulders of the working class as part of their fight for socialism. Again and again he stressed the class struggle which underlay modern Irish history—from the 1798 rebellion, when the Irish landlord class fought its own peasantry, through the Great Famine to the recent Land War, when Parnell the lawyer had betrayed the fight for land.

This was a major contribution to socialist thinking. For at that time the international socialist movement dismissed the idea that the working class might lead such a struggle in colonial or backward countries. Indeed the right wing supported colonialism on the grounds that it was the only way forward for backward countries. The majority of the international socialist movement did not go this far, but their opposition to colonialism focused simply on the atrocities committed by the imperialist powers. Connolly argued that socialists had to champion the fight against colonialism in both the oppressor and the oppressed states.

The other Marxist who had developed similar ideas was the Russian revolutionary Leon Trotsky. He argued that the working class could seize power in Tsarist Russia and other countries where 'normal' capitalist democracy did not exist. He too argued that the capitalist class in such societies was too weak and too scared of the working class to challenge the *status quo*. Further, he argued that Russia, Ireland and other backward countries were linked into the international capitalist economy. A successful workers' revolution in one of these countries could trigger a revolutionary development in the advanced countries of Europe and North America.

In 1917 Trotsky's theory, which he termed 'permanent revolution', was to be brilliantly vindicated when the relatively small Russian working class took power.

Like Lenin and Trotsky, Connolly's Irish Socialist Republican Party stood on the left wing of the international socialist movement. At the international congress of socialist parties in 1900 a split developed over the decision of a member of the French party to join a coalition government with the right. At the congress the right wing, who stood for winning reforms within the existing capitalist state by using its institutions, backed this move. The majority simply condemned it because the individual concerned had failed to consult his party. The ISRP delegates joined with Lenin and the Polish-German revolutionary Rosa Luxemburg in arguing that what was at stake was the choice between reform and revolution.

But by 1903 the ISRP had failed to grow. Irish workers were not fighting back and the potential for winning people to socialist ideas was not great. Connolly decided to emigrate to the United States. There he came into contact with the developing ideas of syndicalism—the belief that socialism was possible only *after* the working class had gained control of the economy through industrial struggle. For the syndicalists what mattered was organising workers into 'one big union'.

At a time when most socialist parties placed their emphasis on simply winning votes and elected positions, this emphasis on workers' own struggles was a powerful draw for Connolly and a generation of the best socialist activists. Connolly became a central leader in the Industrial Workers of the World, a syndicalist union which organised mass strikes of the unskilled workers across America.

When Connolly returned to Ireland in 1910 he saw the possibility of creating 'one big union' in the Irish Transport and General Workers Union, newly created by James Larkin. Larkin himself was a powerful agitator but not a great socialist thinker. As a trade union leader he could be magnificent when workers were fighting back. But he was also pulled by pressure from fellow trade union leaders into accepting compromises with the employers. Larkin himself never fully accepted the need for socialist organisation and had a tendency to operate as a one-man band. In that he was very different from Connolly, and at times tension was evident between the two men.

Connolly's ideas are best represented in his pamphlet **Socialism made easy**. Here he combines the case for socialism, and an explanation of why only the Irish working class could achieve national liberation, with an explanation of his syndicalist views. He argues:

> They who are engaged in building up industrial organisations for the practical purposes of today are at the same time preparing the framework for the future... every fresh shop or factory organised under its banner is a fort wrenched from the control of the capitalist class and manned with the soldiers of the revolution to be held by them for the workers.

He saw the need for a socialist party as secondary, arguing that 'such a body can make propaganda, and good propaganda, for socialist principles, but it can never function as the weapon of an industrially organised working class.' Summarising his argument, he wrote: *'the conquest of political power by the working class waits upon the conquest of economic power*, and must function through the economic organisation.'

In line with this statement and right up till his execution, Connolly's main work was within the ITGWU. The Socialist Party of Ireland, which he also led, received less attention—in line with his view that it was concerned with secondary matters such as making propaganda and fighting elections.

But the belief that the working class could take power by seizing economic control through strong union organisation ignored the existence of the capitalist state. In 1913 the defeat following the Dublin lock-out showed that the capitalist class could call on the state's full power. It also showed the need to build a political alternative to the reformist trade union leaders who had betrayed the workers of Dublin.

Yet this defeat didn't change Connolly's views. He was a product of the times. Among the socialists of the day only Lenin grasped the fact that what was needed was a party grouping revolutionary workers on clear principles which set out the need to intervene in every struggle of the working class. Outside a revolutionary period, revolutionary socialist ideas would be held by only a minority. But this minority was capable of leading the mass of workers in struggle, and in that struggle the old ideas would be replaced with an understanding of the need to challenge the existing capitalist system.

Connolly died before the Bolshevik revolution in Russia. Had he lived to see it, the likelihood is that he would have accepted Lenin's understanding of the need for a revolutionary party, like so many of his syndicalist co-thinkers did at that time. Like Lenin, Trotsky and Rosa Luxemburg, he had opposed the First World War and made clear his break with the leaders of the European socialist parties who lined up with their respective states.

But the defeat after the lock-out, support for the war among demoralised Dublin workers and the collapse of the international socialist movement left Connolly demoralised. In addition he foresaw the partition of Ireland and believed this would help destroy workers' unity.

The only organisation which Connolly could now carry with him fully was the reduced ranks of the Irish Citizens Army. The ITGWU was divided over the issue of the war. Increasingly Connolly believed that a rising by a minority of workers was needed to raise opposition to partition and hopefully spark international resistance to the imperialist war.

It was to that end that he entered the alliance with republicans such as Pearse and Clarke—the alliance which would carry through the Easter Rising of 1916. But as Lenin pointed out, it was premature. A year later and it would have tied into rising opposition to the war across Europe. And unlike Lenin, Connolly had not patiently built a revolutionary party which could respond to that development.

The ITGWU couldn't even vote to condemn its own leader's execution. The Socialist Party of Ireland scarcely existed and had little life independent of the ITGWU. The Citizens Army quickly collapsed after the rising into the new Irish Republican Army, the IRA.

James Connolly was a fine revolutionary, a fine fighter for the workers' cause, an outstanding figure in the international socialist movement. But in the end he left behind no organisation capable of carrying through the argument that Irish independence was inseparable from the struggle for socialism. That explains why today those whose politics are a million miles away from Connolly's can claim him for their own.

The incomplete revolution

THE REPRESSION that followed the Easter Rising raised a wave of popular feeling which brought the republicans greater support. As the death toll mounted in the trenches of Flanders, opposition also grew to the First World War. In 1918 Britain threatened to introduce conscription in Ireland. Thousands flocked to join the Irish Volunteers—soon to be renamed the Irish Republican Army, the IRA.

Arthur Griffith, the leader of Sinn Fein, identified himself with this resurgence of republicanism. Sinn Fein became a republican party and began to win popular support away from the Home Rule Party. Throughout 1917 and 1918 Sinn Fein candidates, many of them jailed for taking part in the Easter Rising, won a string of spectacular by-election victories, toppling Home Rule MPs.

The leadership of the republican movement now rested with Griffith, Eamonn de Valera and Michael Collins, a young civil servant who led the IRA. These men, in many ways political conservatives, were to lead a full-scale struggle against British imperialism. The university lecturer de Valera was even to be found leading landless rural labourers in the seizure of land from the absentee British landlords.

The end of the war brought a general election in which Sinn Fein swept the board, taking 73 out of a total 105 Irish seats. The new MPs immediately set up an illegal parliament in Dublin, *Dail Eireann*. Labour had agreed not to contest the election in order to give Sinn Fein a clear run.

The leadership of the Irish labour movement who had succeeded Connolly no longer saw their task as leading the fight for Irish independence. Instead these trade union officials, who dominated both the Irish TUC and the Labour Party, were simply concerned with gaining more members and a greater vote. At the 1916 Irish Trades Union Congress they led a minute's silence for Connolly *and* for those who had died fighting for the British army on the western front.

While de Valera coined the slogan 'Labour must wait' —meaning that social issues such as jobs and wages must be postponed until the fight for independence had been won—these 'leaders' accepted his argument. This position was in stark contrast to that of Connolly, who had *linked* the question of independence with class issues, bringing together the fight against British imperialism with that against native Irish capitalists. De Valera was in effect calling for class differences to be submerged in order to win the struggle for Irish independence.

The leaders of the Irish labour movement were not revolutionaries like Connolly. They hoped simply for a say in how an independent Ireland might be run. Connolly's failure to build a socialist organisation which could carry on his arguments gave them a clear field to maintain their bureaucratic control of the working class.

In the years before the war Connolly had won a huge audience among the working class for the idea that Irish liberty and the end of capitalist rule could not be separated. The strength of that movement had influenced sections of the radical middle classes. Now the argument that independence had to be gained first, before other issues could be considered, carried the day. The working class was no longer in the lead. Instead they were tailing a movement led by middle-class politicians de Valera, Griffith and Michael Collins.

But all the warning signs were there. Two-thirds of the new MPs were middle-class professionals from the cities—lawyers, doctors and teachers—another quarter were businessmen and the rest farmers. Michael Collins personally vetted the candidates. The composition of the Dail reassured the Irish capitalist class, who now saw little threat from the republicans. Indeed they saw the republican campaign as an opportunity to win a degree of independence from British capitalism for themselves.

In Ulster Sinn Fein agreed to the intervention of the Catholic bishops, who divided up the seats between Sinn Fein and the

Home Rule Party. Joe Devlin was re-elected in West Belfast. To Protestants Sinn Fein looked like another priest-ridden outfit.

But between 1919, when the IRA began its campaign, and 1921, when a treaty was signed with Britain, the republicans led a genuine mass struggle against imperialism. The IRA became a strong guerrilla army, particularly strong in Dublin and the south-west where they drew support from rural labourers and poor farmers.

Britain responded by unleashing a wave of terror. Highly paid former British army officers were recruited into terror squads known as the 'Black and Tans', from the colour of their uniforms. In October 1920 they burnt the city of Cork. In the two years 1920 and 1921 more than 800 houses and 900 shops were destroyed by British forces. Dozens of republican sympathisers were gunned down in cold blood, many more jailed and tortured.

Guerrilla war was accompanied by an increase in working-class militancy. In the four years after 1916 the membership of the ITGWU grew from 5,000 to over 100,000. In April 1918 there was a general stoppage against conscription. February 1919 saw a general strike against military repression in Limerick and one in Belfast for shorter working hours. In May 1920 there was a general strike in support of IRA prisoners and the rail unions refused to move British troops or arms.

In the south-west agricultural labourers began seizing large estates. A wave of occupations spread across the creameries in Munster, the docks of Cork and the Arigna coal mine. While the republican and labour leaders told workers to wait till independence was achieved, there were strong signs that Ireland's revolt might boil over into class war.

In order to win popular support the Dail had adopted a democratic programme which talked abstractly of the ownership of Ireland's land and resources lying with the people. But such rhetoric masked a natural division of interest between propertyless Irish workers—who provided most of the IRA volunteers—and the middle-class members of the Dail. James Connolly's son Roddy described the IRA to a Moscow conference of the world's Communist parties in these words:

> Its membership consists mostly of proletarians and the peasantry, though on the average officered by the younger

members of the petty bourgeoisie and farmers. The majority of the rank and file look upon the establishment of the Irish Republic as of the first importance, and are inclined to defer the solution of social problems to the successful establishment of this aim... The conglomeration of classes comprising Sinn Fein necessarily causes antagonism to develop within the party.

In order to preserve this class alliance the republican movement fought to keep economic questions separate from the fight for independence. In this they relied on the leaders of the labour movement. Within the IRA ranks strict military discipline prevented discussion getting out of hand.

From the left the challenge was faint. The Citizens Army had effectively collapsed into the IRA, or into inactivity. Larkin was in jail in America, while the Irish Communist Party, led by Roddy Connolly, was founded in 1921 too late to influence events.

But as land and factory occupations grew, the republican leadership became concerned. The secretary of the Dail wrote:

> The mind of the people was being diverted from the struggle for freedom by class war... There was a moment when it seemed that nothing could prevent wholesale expropriation.

The success of the Russian Revolution loomed in their minds. Republican courts upheld the property rights of Unionist gentry. In a number of areas IRA units prevented land seizures.

Fear of class war led the republican leadership to explore other ways of gaining some degree of independence. Already Griffith had entered discussions about partition with Unionist politicians from the north, who were worried by a general strike in Belfast in 1919. By the beginning of 1921 both Griffith and de Valera were involved in secret negotiations with the British government. The basis was laid for a treaty involving partition.

For Britain's rulers the treaty removed the Irish question from the country's body politic. The Home Rule question had twice split the British establishment and had become interlinked with other issues, a dangerous factor at a time of increasing class tension. The treaty preserved British economic interests in the Belfast area and guaranteed that the new Irish state would be ruled by safe conservative figures.

Soon the republican movement would split over the shape of the new Ireland. Griffith and Collins reflected the views of capitalist interests which wanted independence but still wanted to retain close economic links with Britain. De Valera wanted a greater degree of independence and closer links with America. Both sides, however, were ready to accept partition, which scarcely figured in the public debates.

The IRA and Sinn Fein split. On the one side stood Griffith and Collins, who won a majority in the Dail and headed the new Irish Free State, created by the treaty with Britain from the 26 southernmost counties of Ireland. In return they recognised Unionist control of the six counties of the north, now separated off. On the other side stood de Valera, leading the opposition to the treaty among the republicans and heading the anti-treaty IRA.

There were now two armies, an intolerable situation for Griffith and Collins, who were determined to secure control over the new state for the Irish capitalist class. If that meant a military confrontation with the republicans, then so be it. Using British guns, the Free State army attacked the IRA's Dublin headquarters.

In the civil war that followed, the republicans had the sympathies of the mass of workers and rural labourers. But de Valera and other republican leaders still hoped for a compromise. In contrast, the new Free State used counter-revolutionary terror in order to 'restore order'. Central IRA leaders were executed and prisoners butchered in cold blood. Thousands of republicans were interned and opposition views were censored.

Despite this the leaders of the labour movement, including the newly returned Larkin, stayed neutral. That did not stop the employers launching their own offensive. Trade union membership slumped by a third and lock-outs enforced wage cuts.

Now that the 'national' struggle had been won, class differences need no longer be submerged. Ireland's new ruling class had brought them back to the surface with a vengeance. When Irish capitalists felt things were going too far, key sections of the republican movement not only called a halt to the struggle but turned on their former allies. They did so not because they were 'rotten republicans' but because they represented different class interests, interests which felt threatened by the possibility of independent working-class organisation or even by too great a break in the economic ties with Britain.

In 1923 de Valera ordered an end to republican resistance. What one republican leader of the 1980s has described as the 'four glorious years', when the IRA challenged British rule, had ended with Connolly's worst fears confirmed. In 1914 he had warned that partition would mean 'a carnival of reaction both North and South, would set back the wheels of progress, would destroy the oncoming unity of the Irish labour movement.' Elsewhere he had also written:

> Such a scheme would destroy the Labour movement by disrupting it. It would perpetuate in a form aggravated in evil the discords now prevalent, and help the Home Rule and Orange capitalists and clerics to keep their rallying cries before the public as the political watchword of the day. In short, it would make division more intense and confusion of ideas and parties more confounded.

It was a warning of what Irish workers would have to endure for the next 60 years or more.

Chapter nine
The mirror states

BOTH NEW IRISH STATES came into existence amid civil war. In the north sectarianism now took even deeper root. But even in the newly independent south, republican opponents of partition found themselves facing repression similar to that across the border.

In Northern Ireland between June 1920 and June 1922 more than 400 people were killed in sectarian violence, the majority of them Catholics. An estimated 23,000 people were left homeless. About 12,000 workers had been driven from their jobs—9000 of these were Catholics, the remainder Protestant socialists and union activists.

The new state of Northern Ireland could rely on sixteen battalions of British troops and 50,000 members of the newly formed RUC and B-Specials. Whole units of the pre-war UVF were recruited into these forces. The Special Powers Act gave the home affairs minister dictatorial powers, including internment without trial, a ban on assemblies, organisations and publications, and even the power to refuse an inquest into the deaths of people killed by the police. Little wonder president Vorster of South Africa later said he 'would be willing to exchange all the legislation [of apartheid]... for one clause of the Northern Ireland Special Powers Act.'

The level of violence was necessary if the new Unionist government was to retain control. More than a third of the new state's population were Catholics. The new border had been drawn to include in the north the greatest possible area that would contain a safe Protestant majority. Three counties of the historic province of Ulster had in fact been excluded, because otherwise the Protestant majority might have been endangered.

Local councils that were under republican control were now simply dissolved. In towns such as Derry and Newry new rigged boundaries were drawn to give the Unionists a majority. Sectarianism was thus built into the new state. Northern Ireland's first prime minister said: 'All I boast is that we have a Protestant parliament for a Protestant people.'

This was to remain true for the next 50 years. Between 1921 and 1969 only three members of the Northern Ireland cabinet were not members of the Orange Lodge. During the 50 years of existence of the Northern Ireland parliament at Stormont only one opposition bill was passed: the Wild Bird Act of 1930! In County Fermanagh, where Catholics were in a majority, they were given just 35 per cent of council housing and 9 per cent of council jobs. In 1943 only 37 out of 634 civil servants were Catholics, with none in the top 85 posts. Catholics were virtually excluded from Belfast's shipyards and major engineering plants.

Sectarianism kept workers divided and the Unionist rulers in power and profit. Protestant workers might have certain minimal advantages over Catholics but they too suffered from the effects of Unionist rule. An examination of Unionist MPs showed that 86 per cent of them were industrialists, managers or major landowners. The Unionist cabinet was simply an executive committee for Northern Ireland's wealthy few.

Even in 1921 Belfast had the highest level of infant mortality in Britain and Ireland. Between 1930 and 1939 unemployment never fell below 20 per cent, reaching a height of nearly 30 per cent. The shipyards shut until orders arrived, while engineering and linen factories laid off thousands of workers. Protestant workers suffered greatly. Even in the boom years of the 1950s unemployment remained high, twice that of Britain, as the linen and other traditional industries collapsed. Wage levels for skilled workers, which before partition had equalled those of British workers, now fell below them.

The beginning of the 1960s saw serious lay-offs in shipbuilding and industry generally. The old Northern Ireland economy was collapsing. In the next 20 years the number of jobs in the shipyards and in heavy engineering would halve. A survey taken in 1960 found 96 per cent of houses on the Protestant Shankill Road without indoor toilets, hot water, bath or washbasin. In the Protestant town of Ballymena nearly half the houses had no running water.

The Unionist regime blocked attempts to introduce reforms that had been granted to British workers. They opposed the welfare state and implemented it only in a 'controlled' way. Abortion and homosexuality remained illegal and measures such as legal aid were blocked. Of course Catholics suffered most in terms of jobs, education and housing, but the point is that it was the Unionist bosses, not Protestant workers, who benefited from the Orange State.

Indeed the Unionists were happy to see the Catholic church operate in the north as a 'state within a state', controlling education, health care and other services in the minority community. Both Unionists and the Catholic hierarchy opposed measures such as comprehensive education and divorce. Abortion remains unobtainable today, even though it was legalised by the British parliament in 1967. (In the south the illegality of abortion is enshrined in the constitution.)

But what alternative did the new state to the south offer workers?

The 1920s saw the Free State ruled by a right-wing government that persecuted republicans and trade unionists alike. The Catholic church was granted 'special status', with control over social policy. Unemployment was high there too and emigration the only alternative. What opposition there was centred on the republicans defeated in the civil war. The Irish Labour Party restricted itself to pleading for reforms to be passed by a government which turned a deaf ear.

De Valera, who led the semi-illegal republicans, began to challenge the policy of Sinn Fein, which refused to participate in the institutions of the southern state. His opponents clung to the belief that military action could achieve an all-Ireland republic. He now argued that there was a 'constitutional' path—which could be opened by winning control of the new state. In 1926 he set up Fianna Fail.

At first the split seemed to be about the choice between military and electoral policies. Fianna Fail took a majority of the republicans' support. Once again de Valera used radical rhetoric in order to win support among the working class and the landless labourers. But behind the rhetoric he represented a key section of the Irish capitalist class.

The Free State economy remained tied to the British market. Industry had not developed to any major degree in the south. De Valera promised to raise import controls in order to protect Irish industry and allow it to develop unchallenged. The world slump of the 1930s hit the south hard. A third of its total trade simply collapsed. For whole sections of Irish capital de Valera seemed to offer a solution. Elsewhere in the world, capitalist states were creating trade barriers to block foreign imports and using state intervention to achieve industrial development. Following their example, de Valera promised state intervention to stimulate growth.

In 1932 de Valera was elected to office. He was supported by the IRA, the Labour Party and even James Larkin, the veteran of 1913. That support meant Fianna Fail could win a majority of working- class votes.

De Valera took the radical step of stopping the compensation payments made by small farmers to their former British landlords. Britain retaliated by banning Irish goods. De Valera responded likewise—and an 'economic war' began. By the time this 'economic war' was over, in 1938, Irish industry had grown significantly, helped by generous state allowances. The state itself took control of transport, the new hydro-electricity industry, the major shipping company and the production of sugar and peat. The 'economic war' didn't solve the problems facing Irish workers, but it did help create a series of Irish-owned companies that gave their backing to Fianna Fail.

Irish neutrality in the Second World War of 1939-45 boosted de Valera's popularity, but the years that followed the war brought recession. During the 1950s half a million people emigrated. Unemployment rose to 90,000.

De Valera also continued to allow the Catholic church a special say in how the country was run. A new constitution recognised this 'special position' and outlawed divorce and contraception. In 1950 the bishops were able to stop the setting up of a free health service for children and mothers on the grounds that it was 'unchristian'.

De Valera's special trick was in combining republican rhetoric at election time with repression against those who were actually fighting partition. IRA members were thrown into solitary confinement, kept naked, interned and during the war years executed by a hangman imported from Britain. In the late 1930s bigoted Catholic mobs burnt down the headquarters of the Communist Party and the left-wing Republican Congress.

Connolly's prediction had come true. A 'carnival of reaction' ruled north and south. In both states the ruling class used the respective ideologies of nationalism and Orangeism to attract working-class support.

Repression: North and south

THE NORTH

1922 CIVIL AUTHORITIES (SPECIAL POWERS) ACT: Allowed arrest without charge, internment without trial, flogging, prohibition of inquests, execution, use of depositions by witnesses as evidence, destruction of buildings, requisitioning of land and property, prohibition of meetings, organisations and publications. Allowed the minister of home affairs to make any measure 'he thinks necessary for the maintenance of order' without consulting parliament and to delegate the Act's powers to whoever he chose.

1923 CIVIL AUTHORITIES (SPECIAL POWERS) ACT: Renewed; renewed each year until 1928, when it was made permanent.

1970 CRIMINAL JUSTICE (TEMPORARY PROVISIONS) ACT: Six-month sentence made mandatory for riotous behaviour.

1971 PAYMENT FOR DEBT ACT: Brought in after a mass rent and rate strike against internment. Allowed removal of money at source from supplementary benefit and other state benefits to cover current rent and any arrears. Later extended to cover gas and electricity bills and to cover deduction from the pay of public employees.

1972 DETENTION OF TERRORISTS ORDER: Attempt to conceal internment without trial by bringing internees before a judicial commissioner.

1973 NORTHERN IRELAND (EMERGENCY PROVISIONS) ACT: Replaced the Special Powers Act. Set up non-jury courts to try those accused of political offences. Gave army power to hold suspects for four hours for questioning, after which they must be released or handed to police for 72 hours further questioning.

1975 PREVENTION OF TERRORISM (SUPPLEMENTARY TEMPORARY PROVISIONS NORTHERN IRELAND) ORDER: Allowed suspects to be held for first 48 hours, then five days, for questioning if secretary of state authorises. Secretary of state can also serve exclusion order on persons not from Northern Ireland, keeping them out of Northern Ireland.

1976 CRIMINAL LAW JURISDICTION ACT: North and South. Allowed trial in one state for offence committed in the other.

1978 NORTHERN IRELAND (EMERGENCY PROVISIONS) ACT: Consolidated earlier legislation and required secretary of state to consult parliament on the introduction of internment—either before or after the event.

THE SOUTH

1922 CONSTITUTION: Articles 6 and 70 allowed for military law and military courts.

1923 PUBLIC SAFETY (EMERGENCY POWERS) ACT: Allowed indefinite internment. Made permanent in 1926, allowing government to introduce a three-month state of emergency.

1927 PUBLIC SAFETY ACT: Allowed detention of suspects for seven days, which might be extended to two months. Allowed proscription of illegal organisations and 'seditious publications'. Set up military courts with a mandatory death sentence for those found guilty of murder or treason. Repealed in 1928.

1931 CONSTITUTION (AMENDMENT NUMBER 17) ACT: Article 2a allowed detention of suspects for 72 hours, proscription of illegal organisations (twelve were immediately banned), and permanent military courts with power of execution.

1937 CONSTITUTION: Article 2a of the 1931 Act and permanent tribunal abolished. Allowed non-jury courts to be set up.

1939 OFFENCES AGAINST THE STATE ACT: Replaced Public Safety Act. Allowed indefinite detention, proscription of organisations. Set up special criminal non-jury court, which sat until 1946.

1939 EMERGENCY POWERS ACT: Allowed internment, arrest of Irish citizens without warrant, censorship. A 1940 amendment extended this to non-Irish citizens and introduced military tribunals. Repealed 1946.

1960 BROADCASTING ACT: Allowed prohibition of broadcasts supporting 'subversion'.

1972 OFFENCES AGAINST THE STATE (AMENDMENT) ACT: Allowed conviction on charge of membership of illegal organisation on the basis of a police chief superintendent's statement. Special criminal non-jury court introduced.

1976 CRIMINAL LAW JURISDICTION ACT: North and South. Allowed trial in one state for offence committed in the other.

1976 EMERGENCY POWERS ACT: Allowed suspects to be held for seven days.

1976 CRIMINAL LAW ACT: Instituted seven-year maximum sentence for membership of an illegal organisation (previously two years maximum), ten years for incitement to join an illegal organisation.

1976 BROADCASTING AUTHORITY (AMENDMENT) ACT: Banned interviews with members of proscribed organisations.

Chapter eleven
Workers against the Unionist monolith

CAN THE HOLD OF UNIONISM over Protestant workers in Northern Ireland be broken?

Republicans and many on the left see the alliance which unites Unionist bosses with Protestant workers as something that cannot be breached. But the Unionist alliance has never been some unbreakable monolith. Again and again it has split on class lines. Indeed what is remarkable is the level of unity that has been shown between Catholic and Protestant workers involved in common struggle.

In the 1907 dock strike Belfast workers had shaken their Unionist bosses. But tragically the strike was betrayed and defeated, and the unity across the religious divide was lost. The Independent Labour Party was unable to confront sectarianism and preserve among a minority of workers the unity shown during the strike.

But at the beginning of 1919 Belfast saw its greatest strike. Spurred on by a strike on Clydeside for shorter hours, 40,000 workers in the shipyards and engineering plants came out on strike for a 44-hour week. The strike was longer and larger than the celebrated stoppage on 'Red Clydeside'. It was run by the Belfast district committee of the engineering union and a majority of its leaders were Catholic, though most strikers were Protestant.

The strike soon spread to electricity workers and the trams. But the engineering union district committee was determined to keep control of the strike. They refused an offer of help from trade unionists in Dublin. When some followers of James Connolly organised meetings they were banned.

Unionist leaders denounced the strike as a 'Sinn Fein,

Bolshevik plot'. The Glasgow strike had collapsed, isolated by the refusal of the engineering union's national leaders to organise solidarity. These same officials also expelled the leaders of the Belfast strike from the union. The authorities now felt confident enough to crush the strike. Troops occupied the power stations, ensuring power supplies. The district committee refused to spread the action to meet this. Faced with the determination of employers and authorities, they eventually ordered a return to work.

But at a time when southern Ireland was on the edge of full-scale guerrilla war and the Unionist machine was in top gear, such solidarity was remarkable.

The unrest continued. On May Day 1919 100,000 workers demonstrated in Belfast. In 1920 building workers won a strike for a 44-hour week and shipyard workers won pay increases. In local elections 97 Labour candidates were returned in the Ulster counties. The **Irish Times**, then a Unionist paper, pointed out there was little basis for partition.

But again there was no socialist organisation prepared to confront sectarianism. The republicans showed no interest in linking with militant Protestant workers. Instead they allowed the Catholic church to impose an agreement in Northern Ireland, sharing out seats with Home Rule Party politicians who were notorious as Catholic bigots.

In July 1920 shipyard employers sacked Catholic workers and union activists for being 'disloyal'. Orange mobs forced some 12,000 workers from their jobs, many of them Protestant trade unionists. Over the next two years sectarian violence grew as a reflection of partition. More than 400 people were killed.

But the recession of the early 1930s once again paved the way for an explosion of militancy by Belfast's workers. More than 70,000 were unemployed and the shipyards shut down. The Unionist government was prepared to pay only a pittance to those who signed on for 'relief' work, laying roads and mending pavements. The Communist Party began to organise among the unemployed, and this agitation united Protestant and Catholic workers. When the Unionist government cut the money paid for relief work the Communist Party felt confident enough to hit back. In September 1932 they called a strike of those workers on relief work. Belfast Trades Council and the Labour Party opposed the strike but flying pickets ensured a total stoppage. Sixty thousand people attended a protest rally and the unemployed began occupying the workhouses, clashing with the RUC.

The Unionist government denounced the strikers and drafted another 700 police into Belfast. A further demonstration was banned. Despite this, tens of thousands demonstrated throughout Belfast, again clashing with the police. The RUC then concentrated on the Catholic Falls Road, hoping to incite a riot and portray it as a republican rebellion in order to re-impose sectarian divisions. The ploy failed. Rioting spread from the Falls to the Protestant Shankill Road.

The government was desperate. But with two of the strike leaders in jail and hundreds more on rioting charges, the union officials who made up Belfast Trades Council intervened. They announced the threat of a general strike in order to gain control of the movement, then organised a compromise agreement which ended the strike.

Contrary to myth, the Belfast IRA played no part in the rioting. In the 1930s it remained deeply conservative, staunchly Catholic and hostile to socialism. In 1921 it had supported the partition settlement and sided with the new Free State government in the civil war.

The following year a rail strike throughout Ireland saw both states use force to try to break the strike. Belfast dockers struck in sympathy and 5000 people attended a strike support rally. The strike, however, was defeated.

Such militancy provoked a split inside the IRA, which was tailing de Valera's Fianna Fail government in the south. In 1934 the left-wing Republican Congress was formed. The Congress established five branches in Belfast—four in Protestant areas. At that year's republican commemoration for Wolfe Tone, the 'father of Irish republicanism', 500 Protestant workers marched behind a banner reading 'Shankill Road Belfast Branch. Break the connection with capitalism. Connolly's message our ideal.' The IRA leadership ordered the banners removed and IRA volunteers charged the Protestant workers.

The next day the Belfast contingent marched through Dublin to Connolly's grave. There a speaker stated:

> We do not pretend to speak on behalf of the majority of Belfast workers. We are a body of Protestant workers, the

vanguard of the working class... [come from Belfast] to pledge our determination at the graveside of Connolly to do all we can to carry out [his] message... to break all connection with England and to smash Irish capitalism.

But the Republican Congress quickly split, for reasons which lay largely outside Ireland. The Communist Party had now switched its position in line with that laid down by Stalin, the Russian leader who now dominated the world Communist movement. Stalin feared the threat to Russia from Germany, where Hitler's Nazis had taken power in 1933. To meet that threat he wanted an alliance with Britain, France and the other 'democracies'. At the founding conference of the Republican Congress a majority of the delegates backed the view that they should aim to create a 'Popular Front'. The struggle for socialism was ruled out. Instead the key task was the defence of Russia and democracy. This meant an alliance with de Valera in the south and 'progressive' Unionists in the north, elements which were expected to support Stalin's call for unity against Hitler.

A minority of the Congress—including Connolly's son and daughter and key former IRA members—opposed this with a clear call for a Workers' Republic. When they were defeated they left the Congress. The Congress itself quickly fell apart. Many of the Protestant workers who had joined it went to fight and die in the Spanish Civil War. Loyalist gangs broke up left-wing meetings and felt confident enough in the summer of 1935 to launch a full-scale pogrom against Catholic families in the Belfast docks area.

Again in 1944, when Unionism was engaged in a war for king and country, Belfast saw another unofficial general strike. Shipyard workers defied a ban on strikes to come out over pay. Within days this spread to 20,000 workers in key war industries. Communist Party union officials unsuccessfully opposed the strike and demanded a return to work. But the Unionist government reacted by jailing five shop stewards. Another 20,000 workers struck in protest. The government then gave in, releasing the men and ordering pay rises.

It has to be stressed that on each of these occasions the explosion of militancy was too short-lived to undermine sectarianism, except temporarily. In particular the absence of any socialist organisation capable of spelling out the lessons and opposing the reformist politicians and union officials meant that each time the Unionist machine regained control.

For class struggle across the sectarian divide could only be built in common struggle against the sectarian state. In 1934 a leading article in the paper **Republican Congress** explained:

> Sectarianism dies out slowly when the fight against it is one of words. Sectarianism burns out quickly when there is team work in common struggle... Those who see in Partition the link between Irish capitalism and imperialist finance, see in the common struggle for the Workers' Republic and the solution of Partition, and in the destruction of exploitation, the withering away of sectarian strife.

Chapter twelve
The civil rights movement

ON 5 OCTOBER 1968 a few hundred demonstrators attempted to march to Derry city centre demanding civil rights in Northern Ireland. After three hundred yards they were stopped by an RUC cordon. Another cordon cut them off behind. The two police cordons then moved simultaneously on the crowd. Men, women and children were clubbed to the ground. A water cannon appeared, forcing the demonstrators back towards the Catholic Bogside district. About a hundred people were later taken to hospital.

The whole thing was shown on television that night. For the first time the reality of Britain's political slum was made known to people outside Northern Ireland. Here was a supposed part of Britain where the police were armed and openly assaulted peaceful protesters.

Here was a place, supposedly as British as the Home Counties, where Unionist businessmen were given extra votes in local government on the basis of what property they owned. Derry itself, with its gerrymandered city boundaries that ensured the Unionists permanent control over a city where Catholics were in a majority, became a symbol for what was wrong in Northern Ireland.

The newly formed civil rights movement took its inspiration from the black movement in the southern states of America. Its leadership came largely from young Catholics influenced by left-wing ideas. But it also reflected the promise of reform that had been made by the Unionist government itself.

By the 1960s Northern Ireland's economy was in deep crisis. The linen industry had collapsed and shipbuilding was in serious decline. In 1963 a new Unionist prime minister took office, former guards officer Terence O'Neill. His aim was to restructure the economy by attracting new industries, reforming local government and modernising transport and housing.

Meanwhile in the south a new Fianna Fail government had decided to develop the southern Irish economy by attracting foreign investment. Generous grants and tax allowances meant that 234 new foreign-owned enterprises had been established by 1965, more than a third of them British-owned. By 1968 southern Ireland was the fifth largest importer of British goods.

The economic basis for partition was being eroded. The Labour government in Britain was pressing for greater collaboration between the two Irish governments, north and south. In 1965 the southern prime minister visited Belfast. The visit was returned and ministers began joint meetings. In this situation open Orange rule in Northern Ireland was something of an embarrassment. O'Neill's government began to talk of change.

But in truth any changes remained in words only. Industrial investment was channelled into the Protestant heartland of Down and Antrim. A new motorway network linked largely Protestant towns in that area. When a second university was created it was centred not in Derry but Protestant Coleraine.

O'Neill himself remained a member of the Orange Lodge. That in itself demonstrated the impossibility of change within the Northern Ireland state. For that state rested on an Orange machine which involved thousands of people, each of them with an interest in seeing that the machine kept its central position in the power structure. There was opposition to O'Neill within his own cabinet. Outside it Ian Paisley began mobilising among the hardliners within the Orange Lodge, the B-Specials and other bodies.

In 1964 O'Neill, under pressure from the right, sent the RUC into the Catholic Falls Road district of Belfast to seize an Irish flag displayed by a republican candidate in a Westminster election. This sparked the worst rioting for 30 years.

O'Neill's reforms were an illusion. In 1967, four years after he took office, his government appointed new members of three public boards running services for all sections of the population. Of 33 members of the youth employment board, three were Catholics; on the hospitals authority two out of 22 were Catholics;

and on the health services board two out of 24. Yet Catholics were more than a third of Northern Ireland's population.

Other factors besides O'Neill's vague talk of change fuelled unrest among Catholic workers. Despite Unionist opposition, British welfare measures such as the National Health Service and free higher education had been introduced in Northern Ireland. These gains simply showed what was lacking in other areas, such as housing.

The march in Derry on 5 October 1968 brought all these pressures to a head. It was followed by other marches. Most ended in confrontation with loyalist counter-demonstrators, led by Ian Paisley and backed up by the police. O'Neill demanded an end to the marches—and this was seized upon by the Catholic middle class. For a while things were quiet.

But the truce was broken in January 1969 by a march from Belfast to Derry organised by socialists active in the civil rights movement. One of the organisers, Eamonn McCann, later wrote in his book **War and an Irish town** that this march 'dredged to the surface all the accumulated filth of 50 Unionist years'. In County Derry police diverted the march into a carefully prepared loyalist ambush. 'A force of some hundreds, marshalled by members of the B-Specials and watched passively by our "escort" of more than a hundred police, attacked with nailed clubs, stones and bicycle chains.' As the march limped into Derry the police attacked the welcoming crowds.

That night the RUC swept into the Bogside. One resident, Mrs Teresa Donnelly, described the scene: 'At a quarter to three in the morning a crowd of police in our street were shouting, "Hey, Hey, we're the Monkees. We'll Monkee you around till your blood is flowing on the ground..." I looked out the window and one shouted, "Come out you Fenian, till we rape you".' Defensive barricades went up throughout the Bogside.

In April tension again mounted as Unionist hardliners ousted O'Neill. In Derry police again attacked the Bogside. Breaking into a house, they beat a Catholic man to death. In August an Orange march in Derry sparked off the third 'Battle of the Bogside'. Violence spread across Northern Ireland.

By now it was clear to the British government in Whitehall that the state in Northern Ireland was in danger of collapse. They sent the British army to shore it up.

Faced with an orgy of state violence, young workers were looking for a way to hit back. In 1969 both the left in Northern Ireland and the republicans were thrown into crisis by this turn of events. In August 1969 the IRA scarcely existed in Northern Ireland. It had few members, fewer arms and was in no position to defend Catholic areas from increasing attacks by the police and loyalist mobs.

Between 1956 and 1962 the IRA had tried to launch a military campaign along Northern Ireland's borders. Helped by southern security forces, the RUC, together with the B-Specials, had contained this campaign and it had spluttered to a halt. This failure prompted the IRA leadership to shift away from the traditional policy which stressed military action as the means to end partition. They grasped that the IRA's failure lay in its isolation from popular support. They now sought to develop a political analysis which could secure such support.

In doing this they drew on the politics of the Communist Party and in particular on Stalin's 'stages theory of revolution'. According to this the first stage was to secure 'bourgeois democracy' in both Irish states. Stage two would be to achieve a united capitalist Ireland. The final, third stage would be the achievement of socialism. This meant that socialist demands, which fitted 'stage three', should not be raised at a time when the struggle was concerned simply with achieving democratic government—the object of 'stage one'.

The result was that by 1969 the IRA leadership had dumped any policy they had of attempting to change partition. Further, they had effectively disarmed the organisation. In August 1969 the slogan appeared in Belfast's Falls Road 'IRA—I Ran Away'.

In January 1970 the IRA split. Figures who had seemed by-passed because they stressed military activity now seemed to be right. In the wake of the RUC attacks on civil rights marchers and the drafting in of British troops they were now arguing that military conflict in Northern Ireland was inevitable, and that the central task was to end partition. Many of these people were in fact right-wing and opposed to what they saw as 'Communist influences' on the official IRA leadership. They left to form the Provisional IRA.

Many on the left have pictured the Provisionals as some right-wing creature which took over and corrupted the civil rights struggle. Nothing could be further from the truth. Within months young militant workers were flooding to join their ranks as it became obvious that military conflict with the British army was inevitable. Many of these had been active in the civil rights movement and influenced by socialist ideas.

Socialists such as Eamonn McCann, Michael Farrell and Bernadette Devlin, who was elected as an MP at Westminster, had been key leaders of the civil rights movement. They could, at the height of events, attract a powerful audience among Catholic workers. But the tragedy was that they could offer no way forward as it became clear that a full-scale confrontation with the state was unfolding in Northern Ireland.

At the beginning of the civil rights campaign they had hoped to win support among Protestant workers. The campaign had included slogans such as 'Orange and Green Tories out' and 'Class war, not Creed war'. In particular they had argued that the middle-class politicians who led the Catholic Nationalist Party were tarred with the same brush as the Unionists. But two factors determined that these left-wingers would be by-passed by events.

Firstly, their political line was unclear, being largely limited to agitating around basic civil rights issues. As Eamonn McCann wrote later:

> In 1968 and 1969 the left and the right, the 'militants' and 'moderates' in the civil rights movement, were united on one point: that partition was irrelevant... The left was, if anything, even more determined than other anti-Unionist groups to 'keep partition out of it'; and for reasons that were not ignoble. The partition issue had for so long been the 'property' of what we regarded as contending Tory factions that the mere mention of it smacked of jingoism.
> The result was that when, in 1969-70, Catholics in Belfast and Derry were, in the literal sense of the word, forced to raise partition, there was no existing organisation for them to turn to naturally. So they created one... The Provisional IRA exists because partition was going to come into it whether or not the right, the left, or anyone else thought this advisable.

The very institutions of the Orange State reflected sectarianism, from the top civil servant and the senior policeman down to the local education officer and the town hall clerk. Raising the question of civil rights challenged their interests. The state could not be reformed. The simple demand for jobs and houses to be granted to Catholic workers ensured confrontation with a state which rested on institutionalised sectarianism.

What was more, such demands could not win support among Protestant workers because the civil rights movement was not offering a programme that aimed to remove the common burden of unemployment, slum housing and low wages. Its demands simply proposed, or seemed to propose, a reallocation of existing resources—which could only be away from Protestant workers.

What gave the Provisionals their edge in the Catholic communities of the north was that their policies centred on the destruction of the state which upheld sectarianism, created unemployment and doled out repression. The enemy was the RUC and the British soldier at the end of your street.

A further weakness was that the civil rights movement did not attempt to go beyond winning reform in the north by also challenging the southern Irish state. In 1968 there was an explosion of unofficial strikes in the south against collaboration between union officials and employers in holding down pay. In 1969 3000 maintenance workers stopped work for five weeks in an unofficial strike. Mass pickets were respected by some 40,000 workers. Such solidarity brought victory despite union officials' advice that workers should cross the picket lines. The opportunity was there to link the struggles in the north and south. But as McCann points out: 'We were not part of a fight *in* the south against the set-up there.' If the civil rights campaign had challenged the class record of *both* states they might have stood a chance of winning Protestant workers. The failure to do so ensured that Protestant workers remained alienated.

The left's second major failing was that they built no independent socialist organisation. They simply operated as the best militants and the best activists. When all-out confrontation blew up they had no clear organisation or strategy. In Belfast Michael Farrell and others did launch a group based largely among students, the People's Democracy, but this operated mainly as a militant ginger group within the civil rights movement. Later, after a sharp decline in membership, it would simply tail the Provisionals.

McCann correctly describes the result:

> The primary reason why the Provisionals *exist* is that 'socialism' as we presented it was shown to be irrelevant. The Provisionals are the inrush which filled the vacuum left by the *absence* of a socialist option.

One other key force was to emerge: the Social Democratic and Labour Party. The SDLP was made up of 'moderates' in the civil rights movement, men such as John Hume and Gerry (now Lord) Fitt. From its inception it has reflected the views of the Dublin government and has been committed to constitutional change. It has thus been a crucial prop in maintaining the Northern Ireland state.

The rise of the Provisionals

THE BRITISH GOVERNMENT had promised reforms when troops were first sent on to the streets of Northern Ireland. But any changes would mean virtually dismantling the state machine—and that they did not want to do, since the state machine safeguarded the rule of the capitalist class. The history of Northern Ireland since 1969 has been the refusal of each successive British government to carry through any real change. And while the Northern Ireland state remains intact so does the working-class division which it has institutionalised.

In 1969 the Labour government promised to disarm the RUC and disband the B-Specials. Today the RUC remains unchanged and is even more heavily armed. The B-Specials were disbanded but only to be replaced by the Ulster Defence Regiment, whose ranks former Specials joined *en masse*.

The government said the troops had been sent in 'to keep the peace'. But in the wake of attacks by loyalist mobs, with the RUC —which had burned down Catholic homes—continuing as before, and with bigots such as Ian Paisley still inciting sectarianism, the Catholic districts of Belfast and Derry started to organise their own defence.

It immediately became clear that the troops were there to prevent this. Before the Provisionals had barely begun to organise, let alone fired a single shot, attempts to organise defence in Catholic areas were being met with repression. In July 1970 the army imposed a curfew on the Lower Falls area of West Belfast. Troops saturated the area and began raiding for weapons. Soldiers smashed up working-class homes. Four civilians were shot dead. The National Council for Civil Liberties stated: 'No proof has ever been offered that those killed were engaged in illegal activities of any kind. Their only "crime" was to come within the sights of a British soldier who shot to kill.' Two Unionist MPs were then taken on a conducted tour of the area by the army.

Up to this point no British soldier had been killed by the IRA. Those who blame the IRA for the violence in Ireland should ask what their own response would be to troops wrecking their homes, shooting their neighbours or escorting bigots on a triumphal tour of their streets. Against armed troops committed to maintaining the Orange State the IRA seemed the only defence. By the beginning of 1971 the Provisionals had begun to hit back.

The Unionists still ran Northern Ireland. Indeed O'Neill and his supporters had been purged from office by hardliners. The new prime minister demanded the introduction of internment without trial for republicans. The British government—now Tory-controlled—decided to use the method which had worked in other colonial situations such as Aden, Malaya and Kenya: full-scale repression.

On 9 August 1971 British troops swept into Catholic areas at 4.30 in the morning. Hundreds of people were dragged off to be interned—imprisoned without trial. Most IRA volunteers escaped the net. Those interned were subject to intolerable physical hardship, including torture, to make them talk. Later a British judge admitted that torture had taken place but said it couldn't be described as torture since those administering pain found no pleasure in doing so!

On the first day of internment nine Catholic civilians, including a priest, were killed by troops. Tens of thousands of Catholic workers began a rent and rates strike, there were massive demonstrations and support for the IRA swelled. Internment guaranteed the Provisionals mass support in Catholic areas.

On 30 January 1972 the British army attempted once more to intimidate Catholic workers in the most brutal way. That day became known as Bloody Sunday. Crack soldiers of the Parachute Regiment opened fire on a civil rights demonstration of 30,000 people in Derry. Thirteen civilians were gunned down in cold blood. Mass demonstrations in protest spread into the south and even on to the streets of Britain. In Dublin the British Embassy was burned down after a mass demonstration. Factories across the south came out on strike. Under pressure, the Dublin government called a nationwide shutdown to mark an official day of mourning. The Derry city coroner, a former major in the British army, declared: 'It was sheer unadulterated murder. It was murder.' The Parachute Regiment commander who had organised the killings was later rewarded with a knighthood.

It was clear that such brutal repression might endanger British interests by spreading the struggle southwards. Moreover working- class areas of Belfast and Derry became 'no go areas' for the British army, presided over by the IRA. The British government did a dramatic U-turn. In March the Stormont regime was suddenly scrapped. Direct rule was imposed from Whitehall.

In the summer of 1972 the British government even went so far as to negotiate with the IRA. Current republican leaders such as Gerry Adams and Martin McGuinness were flown to England, where they were met by top Tories in the flat of a junior cabinet minister. The negotiations broke down after British troops backed Unionists who were trying to prevent Catholics from moving into a housing estate in West Belfast.

The Provisionals believed that the talks indicated a serious commitment by the British government to negotiate a withdrawal from Northern Ireland. But the British politicians were in fact out to exploit the Provisionals' crucial weakness. Although the Provisionals had widespread support among Catholic workers, they had made no attempt to organise this. Their emphasis was on military activity. As a result their organisation remained of necessity secretive, with decisions in the hands of a few. Even in the 'no go areas' no attempt was made to organise popular control of the areas by the working class itself. There was no political organisation.

Support for the Provisionals rested on experience of the British army and the RUC, but most Catholics still voted for the SDLP. As the smoke of battle cleared the SDLP began to exploit this by arguing for protest to be channelled through the existing ruling institutions. In July 1972 the British troops felt confident enough to re-occupy the 'no go areas'. Even worse, within months of Bloody Sunday the Dublin government was able to pass draconian anti-republican laws without any great protest. The Provisionals had ignored organising in the south except as a means of raising cash and direct support for their military effort.

The British government, along with its counterpart in Dublin, now felt confident enough to try its most developed formula for solving the Northern Ireland problem so far. The Unionist Party had split into fragments after the scrapping of Stormont. The British government now hoped to piece together an alliance between the SDLP and 'moderate' Unionists—now led by Brian Faulkner. As a sop to Catholics an 'Irish dimension' was invented, whereby Dublin politicians would be 'consulted' on northern affairs, while in order to appease Protestants tough anti-IRA measures were promised.

This was a strategy which had worked elsewhere. In Cyprus such a 'moderate' alliance had isolated the 'ultras' on both sides of the divide between Greek and Turkish inhabitants. It had also worked in a number of Britain's former African colonies.

In December 1973 agreement was reached between the British and Dublin governments, the SDLP and Faulkner's Unionist allies at a conference at Sunningdale in the English Home Counties. A new Northern Ireland executive was elected which promised power-sharing between the Catholic and Protestant middle classes.

But the whole project was bound to fail. It was an attempt to give a non-sectarian head to a state whose very being was sectarianism. This was impossible without abolishing that state— and none of the signatories of the Sunningdale Agreement intended that. Faulkner was opposed by a majority of Unionists who ruled out any compromise, by Ian Paisley who was winning widespread support, and by paramilitary outfits such as the Ulster Defence Association—which was organising sectarian assassinations of Catholic civilians. These were not peripheral forces. They organised support inside the RUC and the UDR, among the judiciary and the top civil servants and in every layer of the state machine. The British general election of February 1974 saw hard-line Unionists who were opposed to the Sunningdale Agreement sweep the board in Northern Ireland.

In May 1974 the Ulster Workers Council, which grouped shop stewards in key industries together with paramilitary organisations and hard-line Unionists, called a general strike against the power-sharing executive. Many on the left have argued that the Ulster Workers Council strike only succeeded through mass intimidation. Of course there was intimidation. In Belfast all buses stopped after a working driver was shot dead.

But this cannot explain the success of what was in reality a mass strike, albeit a reactionary one.

Both the RUC and the army looked on as the strike spread. As it became clear that the strike could succeed and that the British government—now Labour once more—was sitting back, support mushroomed. The British TUC general secretary attempted to lead a back-to-work movement. The response was tiny. Northern Irish union officials had to be moved around by army helicopter because strikers ensured they had no petrol.

The crunch came as fuel supplies dried up and the strike spread to the power stations. The Labour government instructed the army to move into the power stations and break the strike. Army commanders refused. The idea that the British army is under the control of the democratically elected government counted for nothing. Army chiefs saw the Protestant paramilitaries, who were involved in the strike they were being asked to break, as a force that could counter the IRA. Instead of a political solution such as power-sharing they wanted a clear hand in dealing with the Provisionals.

Faced with the army's refusal, the Labour government backed down. All this fuelled the confidence of the strikers. Faulkner's support had evaporated. The Labour government told him to resign. Power-sharing was brought to a swift end. The British government was committed to preserving the Orange State.

There was now deadlock. Among Protestant workers it was the likes of Ian Paisley who held sway. Among Catholic workers it was clear nothing had changed. The IRA retained sufficient support for its military campaign.

The Labour government in London had no solution except to try to contain the IRA within the Catholic ghettos. Talk now switched from finding a solution to 'finding a suitable level of violence'. The policies now implemented were those advocated by the army's 'counter-insurgency' experts.

First a policy of 'Ulsterisation' was adopted: running down the number of British troops and replacing them with the RUC and UDR. By 1977 these forces had more than 20,000 members and had been massively re-equipped. This policy continues today. It has been used to try to portray the troubles in Northern Ireland as simply between fellow Irish, in which the British play only a minor role.

The second plank of the new policy was an attempt to paint the republican struggle as merely criminal and nothing to do with the struggle for civil rights. The army now believed that internment had been a mistake. Rather than deal with the IRA by military measures it would be more effective to use criminal law. British ministers began stressing that what was at stake in Northern Ireland was simply the 'rule of law', threatened by a few gunmen, 'godfathers of crime'.

Of course to make 'law and order' work, a new series of 'exceptional' laws was needed, plus the support of the sectarian state apparatus. The whole system of 'justice' that now applies in Northern Ireland was created by the Labour government between 1975 and 1979 to fit this requirement.

Today in Northern Ireland 'Diplock courts' (named after the English judge who proposed them) sit without a jury to try political prisoners. They secure a conviction rate of between 90 and 95 per cent. A confession to police, written or verbal, is sufficient to secure conviction. Under British law the prosecution has to prove that the confession was given voluntarily. In Northern Ireland the defence has to prove torture, inhuman or degrading treatment to get a confession dismissed in court. Suspects can be held for up to a week without charge, in isolation in special interrogation centres. In June 1978 Amnesty International reported that 'maltreatment' was taking place frequently. The following year a police surgeon revealed that he had dealt with 150 people injured during interrogation. An official government report had to admit cases of 'ill treatment'.

Once charged, republicans can find themselves jailed for a year awaiting trial—so the mere charge, whether you're innocent or guilty of any offence, carries a year's prison sentence.

The whole system is presided over by an Orange judiciary. During the 1980s the Lord Chief Justice of Northern Ireland was the son of a Unionist MP and leading Orangeman. He was himself formerly an officer in British military intelligence.

In 1975 the Labour government announced that it was withdrawing political status for political prisoners. Previously they had been allowed to wear their own uniforms, control their own work and education rotas and associate together freely. After 1975 prisoners were placed in high-security 'H-Blocks' within Long Kesh prison camp, later renamed The Maze. Prisoners were now locked in cells, told to wear prison uniform, and granted no special status. This was a key element in the portrayal of the Provisionals as simply criminals.

Republican prisoners hit back by refusing to wear prison uniform or carry out duties. Locked in their cells, they were clad only in a blanket. They then escalated the protest by refusing to wash their cells. The protest spread to women prisoners in Armagh jail.

Virtually every Catholic working-class family in Northern Ireland had had a close friend or relative in jail for political offences. Refusal of political status affected everyone. In particular it became the symbol for everything that was wrong in Northern Ireland—the repression, discrimination and poverty. Starting with relatives of the protesting prisoners, demonstrations began to grow.

At the end of 1980 a hunger strike began among republican prisoners for the return of political status. It was called off when the British government—now the Tories again, led by Margaret Thatcher—seemed to grant some compromise. It began again when it became clear that nothing was on offer. In May 1981 Bobby Sands died on hunger strike. Support for his stand had already been shown by his election as MP for Fermanagh and South Tyrone. Some 100,000 people attended his funeral. In the south a number of factories walked out.

But prime minister Margaret Thatcher made it clear there would be no compromise. She was backed by the Labour Party, which sent a representative, Don Concannon, to tell the dying Sands they wouldn't support him. Nine others died on hunger strike before it was called off. Two prisoners were elected to the Dublin government, while a republican candidate held Bobby Sands' seat at the by-election that followed his death. The hunger strike ensured that the Provisionals received a massive increase in support, despite its defeat. Within two years they would win 40 per cent of the Catholic vote in Northern Ireland. The IRA continued its struggle.

A British army document captured by the IRA in 1979 summed up the situation as it largely remains today:

The Provisional IRA is essentially a working-class organisation based in the ghetto areas of the cities and the rural poorer areas... Our evidence of the calibre of the rank-and-file terrorists does not support the view that they are mindless hooligans... The movement will retain popular support... The Provisional IRA has the dedication and the sinews of war to raise violence intermittently to at least the level of early 1978, certainly for the foreseeable future.

The document warns:

The campaign of violence is likely to continue while the British remain in Northern Ireland.

Chapter fourteen
Under the Thatcher regime

AT THE END OF 1985 the Westminster and Dublin governments signed the Anglo-Irish Agreement with the enthusiastic backing of the SDLP and, after some carefully phrased expressions of concern, Fianna Fail. The agreement, it was claimed, promised a new deal for the Catholic population of the north. The Dublin government and the SDLP bragged about the changes it would bring. In fact the 'reforms' on offer altered nothing fundamental. Much of the agreement was window-dressing. The Irish flag was allowed to be flown legally in the north. Gaelic might be heard at some unearthly hour on television. When the Dublin government demanded that three judges instead of just one should preside over the non-jury Diplock courts, the Lord Chief Justice of Northern Ireland threatened to resign, and the proposal was unceremoniously rejected by Britain after the Tory Lord Chancellor made his opposition clear. Talk of a massive injection of American cash into Northern Ireland's ailing economy came to naught.

The centre of the agreement was a tightening of repression. Some £200 million was added to Britain's security bill. A string of Vietnam-like observation posts was set up along the border between north and south. The Dublin government began extraditing republicans to the north.

The agreement reflected the fact that the ruling class in the south was Britain's chief ally in policing the northern crisis. That alone drove the Unionists into opposition. In order to undercut electoral support for the Provisionals, the agreement set out to give the representatives of the Catholic middle class, the SDLP, some say in how Northern Ireland was run. That again increased

Unionist opposition. But despite Unionist talk of betrayal, the Northern Ireland Secretary Tom King got it right when he told the Unionists 'nothing has changed'.

Throughout 1986 the Unionists banded together to protest against the agreement. One of the changes Catholics had been promised was that 'provocative' Orange marches would not be allowed through their areas. In Portadown the army actually blocked off the Catholic Tunnel area to the Orangemen, sparking rioting. But to make up for that the army escorted an Orange march, led by Ian Paisley, through the town's largest Catholic estate, standing by while Catholic homes were stoned. Tom King went on television to point out that 99 per cent of Orange marches proceeded as usual with no change of route.

A loyalist one-day strike was held in March 1986, held together by massive intimidation. The security forces watched while loyalists blocked 155 roads, including the main highway from the north to Dublin. There were just 57 arrests, despite 132 official complaints of intimidation.

But the Unionists were trapped. They could riot on the streets, but the security forces they were attacking were the very people who were holding down the Catholic population. They could protest against the British government but in the final analysis it was the British government that maintained partition and the Orange state. The Unionists could agree on their opposition to the Anglo-Irish Agreement but on nothing else. Some wanted a return to Unionist rule, some wanted the six counties to be integrated into Britain and some wanted independence for a new Northern Ireland state.

The material basis for partition and Unionism had been undermined by the economic rundown of Northern Ireland. Unionism holds no solution for this. The once hegemonic Unionist Party has splintered into a myriad of warring outfits. Britain might rely on Unionist ideas to guarantee cannon fodder for the RUC and UDR, but it no longer relies on the Unionists to run Northern Ireland. For above all they have no support among the British ruling class. The old Conservative-Unionist alliance, which had fought home rule 70 years earlier, is long gone. In Whitehall they were regarded as foreigners, as Irish, who should accept what was decided for them.

Hopes of a repeat of the 1974 Ulster Workers Council strike

had been sapped by the rundown of the Northern Ireland economy and the stark reality that it depended on British subsidies. In this situation the protests died away. The Unionists went with their tails between their legs to discuss their acceptance of the agreement.

Who paid the price for all this? Ordinary Catholics, who loyalist gangs began murdering in time-honoured fashion. On May 1986 Margaret Caulfield was shot dead beside her husband. Her crime? She was a Protestant who had married a Catholic and lived in a Protestant estate. In Lisburn, North Belfast and other areas Catholics were driven from their homes. One woman described how her home was attacked by masked loyalists:

> They surrounded and bombarded my house. I had the children in the bathroom... There were two RUC jeeps outside and I phoned the police three times but they just sat and watched.

The few Catholics employed at Shorts engineering plant received death threats. Two Orange marches were held right in the factory grounds, while the shopfloor was festooned with loyalist flags and emblems. When publicity in the United States forced the management to take these down the workforce walked out. Management hurriedly agreed that the British Union Jack would fly permanently over the factory, loyalist posters could be displayed in designated areas and pictures of the queen could be put up on machinery.

But amidst a summer of sectarian violence there was one shining ray of hope. In Lisburn a loyalist murder gang threatened Catholics employed in the local health and social security office. The workforce—both Protestant and Catholic—walked out and said they would stay out until the threat was withdrawn. The strike spread spontaneously to 14 other offices in the north. With 1500 people on strike the threat was withdrawn.

The SDLP had received an electoral boost with the promise of reforms. When Unionist MPs resigned in order to force a series of protest by-elections, the SDLP registered a 10 per cent increase in their vote and had a new MP elected.

But hopes that the Provisionals could be marginalised by the Anglo-Irish Agreement were a pipe-dream. The continued daily experience of poverty, repression and sectarianism ensured their support in the Catholic ghettos.

Early in 1987 the deputy chief constable of Manchester police, John Stalker, was suspended from heading an inquiry into three killings by the RUC. Stalker was subjected to a smear campaign orchestrated by the British intelligence service. His crime? He had conducted the inquiry honestly and discovered a shoot-to-kill policy against unarmed republicans. It was a policy sanctioned at the highest level. In the three shootings which Stalker was investigating, a special RUC squad had carried out the killings after British intelligence, MI5, had staked out the victims—in one instance in collaboration with the southern Irish police. Stalker had revealed a cover-up which began with the head of the RUC. The inquiry was halted and Stalker driven from his job.

The British army guaranteed continuing resistance in the Catholic ghettos by a policy of breaking up republican funerals. In one macabre case, which made primetime American television news, they even prevented the funeral taking place.

In May 1987 the elite of the British army, the SAS, provided proof that the Anglo-Irish Agreement was about tougher security. At Loughall they staked out and killed eight IRA volunteers—the biggest single IRA loss since 1921. The killings were applauded by the British media. The leader of the Labour Party, Neil Kinnock, chipped in to congratulate the SAS and announce that this was 'a significant victory against the men of violence'.

With the Anglo-Irish Agreement in her belt, Margaret Thatcher felt confident enough to tighten the screw further. At the beginning of 1988 a Sinn Fein election worker and shop steward, Aidan McAnespie, was crossing a border checkpoint to play Gaelic football. He was gunned down in cold blood. He made the crossing every day, and had been threatened by soldiers. His sister commented: 'He knew it was coming. They told him often enough.' McAnespie's killer, guardsman David Hilden, was given an undisclosed fine for the 'negligent discharge' of his weapon and put back on active service.

At the same time British justice was shown in all its glory when six transparently innocent men, who had been convicted of the 1974 Birmingham pub bombings on the basis of confessions that evidence had shown had been beaten out of them, had their appeal against conviction rejected.

Then on Sunday 6 March 1988 the Ministry of Defence in London issued the following statement:

A suspected bomb has been found in Gibraltar and three suspects have been shot by civilian police.

A few hours later this was expanded:

Security forces were involved in the shootings and military personnel dealt with a suspect bomb.

The following morning a government minister stated that a large bomb had been defused. Newspapers reported the existence of a 500lb bomb, some reported that the suspects had been armed and that there had been a 'shoot-out'.

Then, 24 hours after the killings, British foreign secretary Geoffrey Howe told the House of Commons that there was no bomb in Gibraltar, there had been no defusing, and that the three had been unarmed and trying to leave Gibraltar when they had been shot. This did not stop the Labour spokesperson, George Robertson, speaking immediately afterwards, from congratulating the security forces on the killings, announcing: 'The very fact that this enormous potential bomb was placed opposite both an old folks' home and a school underlines the cynical hypocrisy of the IRA.' He then said of the killings: 'We have got to be glad about it.'

The killings had been carried out by an SAS squad who had been flown into Gibraltar just hours earlier and were flown out minutes after they had completed their task. The justification given for the killings was that the three suspects had become uneasy on being challenged, had turned round and had seemed by their movements to be about either to pull guns or to trigger a remote-control bomb.

It emerged that the British intelligence service MI5 and the Spanish security services had had advance information about a bomb plot, had tailed the three IRA suspects since their arrival in Spain, and had followed them into Gibraltar knowing that they were on a reconnaissance mission and had no bomb. This was revealed by Thames Television, in a programme titled 'Death on the Rock', which also produced witnesses that two of the three had had their hands in the air when shot, and had then been shot again as they lay on the ground.

The British government demanded that the programme broadcast be cancelled. When this failed, the press attacked the witnesses—one was slandered by the **Sun**, which claimed she was a prostitute. In the event the government survived the inquest by the narrowest of margins—after crucial evidence had been withheld and with a jury selected from the population of a tiny colony that had been intimately connected with the British armed forces for centuries past.

The year 1988 also saw further erosion of civil liberties. The Thatcher government removed the right to silence from suspects held in Northern Ireland (this was later extended to Britain) and banned the broadcasting of interviews with republicans. This led to instructions from the BBC that crowd chants at football matches played by Glasgow Celtic should be blotted out and the banning by one radio station of a record by the top-selling Pogues pop group!

On the first anniversary of this media ban the truth about British justice was once again revealed, this time at the Old Bailey, the very heart of the British legal system. After 15 years in British jails three innocent Irish men and one woman—Paul Hill, Gerard Conlon, Patrick Armstrong and Carole Richardson—were set free. They had been convicted of planting a bomb in a soldiers' pub in Guildford, convicted despite the fact that a captured IRA active service unit—the Balcombe Street Four—had admitted to the bombing in open court, convicted despite the fact that they were hardly typical IRA volunteers, being involved in gambling and drugs while openly frequenting Irish pubs in the Kilburn area of London.

In January 1987 the Tory home secretary Douglas Hurd had refused an appeal for a retrial for the Guildford Four, claiming that there was no new evidence. This was a lie. New alibis had emerged for both Paul Hill and Carole Richardson. But his cover-up failed. In October 1989 Lord Justice Lane told the Old Bailey: 'There is no doubt that police officers seriously misled the court. In fact they lied.' There was evidence that the police had fabricated interviews and confessions.

The Guildford Four went free. The British establishment, faced with a flood of new evidence, did not dare let the case drag through the appeal court. Accepting this blow to the credibility of British justice, they decided on a damage-limitation exercise.

This was hardly surprising. Peter Imbert, the head of the Scotland Yard bomb squad in 1974, had been part of the police interrogation team and had interviewed Paul Hill twice immediately after his arrest. No record now exists of what took place at these interviews. By the time of Paul Hill's release Imbert was head of London's Metropolitan Police. The man who had led the prosecution at the trial was Michael Havers. He had told the jury that Gerard Conlon had no alibi. This was a lie. Havers had gone on to become attorney-general in Margaret Thatcher's cabinet. The trial judge, John Donaldson, had risen to become Master of the Rolls.

If the case had been allowed to go to the court of appeal, these three pillars of the establishment would have had to appear in the witness box. They would have had to explain why evidence of Gerard Conlon's alibi, known to the police, had been kept from his defending solicitors until 1989. They would have had to explain why the Director of Public Prosecutions had ignored recommendations that the Balcombe Street Four, arrested in 1977, should be tried for the Guildford bombing which they admitted carrying out. They would have had to explain why the Avon and Somerset police, given the task of investigating new evidence, had suppressed a statement by a police surgeon that he had administered a dose of the drug pethidine to Carole Richardson, who had a serious drug habit, just before she made the 'confession' which was used to convict her.

Paul Hill had spent 1462 days, that's four years, of his 15 years in jail in solitary confinement. He had been moved between prisons 51 times. When he was released, he was clear why he had been in jail: 'as an example to the Irish community,' he said, 'as a method of terrorising the Irish community.' He had been the first person to be held under the Prevention of Terrorism Act, which allows suspects to be held by police for up to a week without charge. The British government had used the public hysteria at the time of the Birmingham and Guildford pub bombings to rush this Act through parliament. They had used the jailing of innocent Irish men and women to intimidate the Irish community in Britain from voicing their opposition to Britain's presence in Ireland.

Despite the release of the Guildford Four, the British ruling class has not changed its policy towards Northern Ireland in any way. The day after the four were released, Britain was found guilty of breaking the European Convention on Human Rights by holding suspects under the Prevention of Terrorism Act for up to seven days without access to a solicitor. The Tory government calmly stated that it would ignore this ruling.

Prime minister Thatcher is a supporter of the death penalty. She was out of the country at the time of the release of the Guildford Four. On her return it was pointed out to her that had the death penalty been in force at the time of their conviction, the Guildford defendants, now proved innocent, would have been hanged. She replied coldly: 'My view is the same. I believe the death penalty should be available...'

Above all the government made it clear that the six men jailed for the Birmingham bombings would remain in jail—even though they too were convicted on the basis of confessions which were beaten out of them and on forensic evidence since disproved. (At the time this book was going to press, there were signs they might yet be forced to release the six).

These events, just recent chapters in a continuing story of repression, fuel support for the Provisionals. Paul Hill was interviewed on Irish radio after his release:

> *Interviewer*: I think probably what people are trying to get from you is whether you sympathise with the IRA or whether you would abhor the kind of violence that...
> *Hill*: Well, if there wasn't an artificial state imposed on my country I wouldn't be here.
> *Interviewer*: You're saying that if there wasn't, none of your misfortunes would have befallen you?
> *Hill*: Of course it wouldn't, and many before me.
> *Interviewer*: So you say that one thing begs the other?
> *Hill*: Of course it does. This epitomises the whole of British dealings with the Northern Ireland problem, the contempt with which they treat Northern Ireland people.

In November 1989 Northern Ireland secretary Peter Brooke echoed the army report of 1979 concerning the IRA, saying:

> It is difficult to imagine a military defeat of such a force, because of the circumstances under which they operate, though the security forces can exercise a policy of containment...

When Brooke admitted that negotiations with the republicans could not be ruled out, the interviewer commented:

> That is quite an admission on the part of the government, that they would in fact consider speaking to the Gerry Adams and Danny Morrisons of this world.

Brooke replied:

> Let me remind you of the move towards independence in Cyprus, and a British minister stood up in the House of Commons and used the word 'never' in a way which within two years there had been a retreat from that word.

This is a sharp reminder that the British ruling class views Northern Ireland simply as a colonial problem.

Chapter fifteen

Can the Provisionals win?

THE PROVISIONALS were the product of British policy in Northern Ireland. From the Lower Falls curfew in 1970, internment and Bloody Sunday, the hunger strikes of 1981 and beyond, the British government has ensured that the Provisionals retain a high level of support in the Catholic working-class ghettos.

Socialists must start by making it clear that they are with the Provisionals against the British army. The army is in Northern Ireland to maintain a sectarian state. It arms sectarian paramilitary forces such as the RUC and UDR. It presides over a legal system which ensures that any form of political protest is treated as criminal. Above all, it protects the interests of a ruling class that has given workers in Northern Ireland, both Protestant and Catholic, the highest unemployment and the poorest housing in western Europe.

Unfortunately sections of the left in both Ireland and Britain have echoed the hysterical claims of the British government that the Provisionals are responsible for the divisions and the killings in Northern Ireland. In Ireland the Workers Party—the former Official republicans—concentrates on denouncing the Provisionals. In Britain sections of the Labour Party, both on the right and the left, regularly denounce the Provisionals.

While British troops remain in Northern Ireland, the sectarian state remains and the violence will continue. The responsibility for this does not lie with the Provisionals but with British politicians, both Labour and Tory, with the Dublin government, and with the bigots who still run Northern Ireland.

However, while socialists defend the Provisionals, that does not mean that we believe that they can lead the struggle to success and that the job of socialists is merely to cheer them on. A few hundred IRA volunteers, however courageous, cannot militarily defeat 10,000 British troops, 20,000 armed police, and the Ulster Defence Regiment, when they have the southern Irish state also lined up against them. In Northern Ireland today there are half a million Catholics, a third of the population. Overall they are one-seventh of Ireland's total population. That minority cannot alone undo the partition on which both Irish states rest, a division which both states will do their utmost to maintain.

The limits of the struggle by Catholic workers in Northern Ireland have been revealed at each high point of the 'troubles'.

In 1969 the explosion in the Catholic ghettos could bring British troops in to replace the RUC and B-Specials; it could win promises of reforms; but it could not ensure that those reforms were made (they weren't); it could not prevent the troops taking over the role of the RUC and B-Specials; nor could it bring down the Orange state.

At the time of internment and Bloody Sunday in 1972 the whole Catholic population took to the streets. The Provisionals became the most effective guerrilla force any developed country had seen. But again this could not end partition. The scrapping of Stormont and the imposition of direct rule from Westminster defused the situation by removing what people saw as the symbol of oppression. The oppression itself remained.

In 1981 the Catholic population again united behind the hunger strikers. Again thousands marched and rioted. But the protest remained confined in the ghettos. In that situation Catholic workers did not have the means to combat repression, nor even to ensure that the hunger strikers did not die.

Yet the Provisionals retain their support. They remain the one force which directly opposes a system that doles out unemployment, slum housing and repression to Catholic workers. To understand why the Provisionals are unable to achieve success we need to examine their politics. For as they themselves make clear, they come from a distinct political tradition: two centuries of Irish republicanism.

One thing is different today: for the first time ever republicanism has its base among the urban working class. This has been reflected in a significant move leftwards in the language and aims of the Provisionals. Nevertheless, republicanism still sees its prime aim, above everything else, as Irish independence from Britain.

Yet the tradition of republicanism leads the Provisionals to policies which cannot break the deadlock in the north. For every member of the Provisionals the emphasis still lies on the 'cutting edge of the IRA'—the military effort to topple the northern state. This remains true whether or not individual members of the Provisionals regard themselves as socialists. Of necessity their main stress must be on the secret operations which involve a few hundred volunteers. Street demonstrations, rallies and the like are seen as secondary: their main importance lies in how they can further the armed struggle.

In 1972, when the leaders of the Provisionals were flown to London for talks with the British government, they believed military victory was within their grasp. Such claims were repeated in 1975 when contacts were resumed between the Provisional leadership and top British civil servants. But by the late 1970s a new generation of Provisionals had grasped that military victory was not achievable in the short term. They understood that they would have to organise their support in the Catholic ghettos. They grasped too that failure to organise in the south gave the Dublin government a free hand in dealing with them. At times of crisis politicians in the south might trot out a few phrases attacking the northern state, but a few weeks later they would feel able to continue their repression of republican supporters.

In the wake of the 1981 hunger strikes a new leadership took over, grouped around Gerry Adams, Danny Morrison and Martin McGuinness—men with a left-wing reputation. There had been electoral successes during the hunger strikes, not least Bobby Sands' election to parliament at Westminster. Now, in order to win popular support, the new leadership urged republicans to turn to electoral policies in both the north and the south.

But this was no rejection of the military struggle. On that point they were plain: the new strategy was based on 'the Armalite *and* the ballot box'. The Provisionals now saw their struggle, to use Gerry Adams' own words, as 'a long war—lasting 15, 20 or even 30 years'. If the IRA can keep up its campaign, they argued, over a period of time the cost of maintaining Northern Ireland will prove too great for the British government. The new electoral strategy remained secondary to the armed struggle. As Danny

Morrison told an interviewer in September 1984:

> The thing I have to emphasise, that all republicans are united on, is that electoral policies will not remove the British from Ireland. Only armed struggle will do that.

How could the armed struggle succeed? In October 1984 the Provisionals bombed the hotel in Brighton where the Tory cabinet was gathered for the annual party conference. Prime minister Margaret Thatcher and her colleagues had a narrow escape. Morrison told the **Observer** newspaper:

> If that bomb had killed the British cabinet, examine then what would have happened. There would have been a rethink within British political circles and it probably would have led to a British withdrawal in a much shorter period. It would have been unique in British constitutional history, apart maybe from Guy Fawkes.

Yet republican bombs have already killed a member of the British royal family, Lord Mountbatten, and a Tory cabinet minister and close friend of Margaret Thatcher, Airey Neave. Do these seem to have brought the British government any closer to withdrawing the troops from the north? There is no sign of it.

The British government is implementing policies in Northern Ireland which reflect the interests of the ruling *class*—and not just that in Britain. In Ireland today, north and south, all sections of the ruling class and the bulk of the middle class—Catholic and Protestant—are determined to maintain the *status quo*. And this stance is supported internationally, as US presidents Reagan and then Bush have made clear in Washington. Even killing the British cabinet would not change that. The coalition of class forces which opposes the Provisionals would remain intact.

In fact the Provisionals' own policies reflect the class forces that stand against them. Today Provisional leaders talk of a 'democratic socialist republic'. They pay lip-service to issues such as women's liberation. This new 'left-wing' leadership reflects the fact that for the first time republicanism is based among the urban working class, in an Ireland where the other classes oppose any major changes.

The election results achieved by the Provisionals, through their political organisation Sinn Fein, show this. The Catholic community is divided between those who back the Provisionals, centred on the working class of the ghettos and the poor rural areas, and those who continue to back the SDLP, centred on the Catholic middle class. In the British general election of 1983 the Provisionals won 13.4 per cent of the votes in Northern Ireland, compared to the SDLP's 17.9 per cent. Later that year John Hume of the SDLP outpolled Danny Morrison in the elections for the European parliament, polling 151,399 votes to Morrison's 91,476 across Northern Ireland. In the 1985 local elections the Provisionals again won around 35 per cent of the Catholic vote in Northern Ireland, again tailing the SDLP. In June 1989 their vote held up in the local elections but was almost halved in the European elections, reflecting the fact that the Sinn Fein candidate had no hope of defeating Hume.

In the south, Adams has been clear that the Provisionals cannot win support simply because British troops are kicking in doors on the Falls Road in Belfast. Instead he cites the success of the Workers Party in winning electoral support, arguing that the Provisionals must combine a 'correct attitude to the national question with the groundwork the Workers Party have been doing'. Yet the Workers Party operates in an identical way to the European socialist and labour parties. They stand for change *within* the existing institutions of society. They argue that workers can change things only by electing representatives capable of achieving reforms for them, not through any action of their own.

In Belfast, Derry and now Dublin the Provisionals have set up constituency advice centres in the style of the established parties, ensuring house repairs are done and benefits claimed. This work is of course valuable to residents of the inner cities but it does not develop independent organisation of the working class. Instead the stress is all on what elected representatives can achieve on behalf of their constituents.

Electoral success won't force the British government to back down. Gerry Adams, Danny Morrison and other key republicans in fact accept this. They argue that electioneering allows them to organise popular support for the IRA's armed struggle.

The limits of the Provisionals' commitment to 'socialism' remain clear too. When Adams was asked about his socialist ideas in 1979 he replied: 'We genuinely believe that when the struggle for independence is completed and the democratic process re-established, the best solution is decentralised socialism and government structures.' So he has set out clearly the order of priorities: *first* the struggle for independence has to be won, *then* they will think about socialism. Not only that, but workers' action too is subordinated to the military struggle: workers can help, not by fighting for their own interests against their employers, but by giving support to the Provisionals.

At every point, policies are judged by their ability to win support for the armed struggle. Thus Adams rushed to assure Irish Americans that: 'There is no Marxist influence within Sinn Fein. I know of no one within Sinn Fein who is a Marxist or who could be influenced by Marxism.' That was in 1979. Adams repeated it in 1985. The reason? There had been a campaign by the US government to scare off Irish Americans, right-wing in the main, from giving money to the Provisionals by portraying them as 'Marxist terrorists'.

Fundamentally, the Provisionals believe they can unite a majority of the Irish people across class lines. During the hunger strikes of 1981 the Provisionals tried to mobilise Fianna Fail MPs (who then sat in government in Dublin), SDLP councillors and Catholic bishops. Their newspaper **An Phoblacht** declared: 'Britain can be beaten when the Free State premier, the SDLP leaders and the Catholic hierarchy are forced to apply their muscle instead of as at present playing at it.' But the people listed are the Irish ruling class. Despite their nationalist rhetoric they will not act against the interests of their class by backing the Provisionals.

Gerry Adams, in his book **The Politics of Irish Freedom** which was published in 1987, rejects a class analysis of the Irish struggle. Socialism, we are told, is not yet on 'the historical agenda'. It would be 'ultra-left' to be 'putting forward "socialist" demands that have no possibility of being achieved until real independence is won'. This is an argument which seems to echo de Valera's position in 1918: that 'Labour must wait'.

Adams goes on to say that: 'Identifying only with sections of the working class... is not enough. We need unity against imperialism, against one enemy and in one struggle.' But unity with whom? Adams gives the answer when he quotes approvingly a member of Fianna Fail who said that Sinn Fein and Fianna Fail were 'second cousins'. On the birth of both the Provisionals and the SDLP he writes: 'It might have been better if there could have been some kind of general unity, in which both parties would agree to disagree on social and economic issues and maximise pressure on points of agreement.'

In 1985 Provisional leaders urged 'pan-nationalist' unity with the SDLP in the Northern Ireland local council elections. After the elections they entered into coalitions with the SDLP on several councils where they had a combined majority. But the SDLP is the voice in the north of the Dublin government and, by its willingness to share power with the Unionists, a major prop of the northern state. The Anglo-Irish Agreement was designed to strengthen this prop.

When the Unionists resigned their seats over the agreement and forced a series of by-elections, the Provisionals asked the SDLP to discuss an electoral pact. The SDLP was championing the agreement, which was aimed against the Provisionals, so on what basis could there be any electoral pact? This was followed by appeals for a summit meeting between Gerry Adams and the Fianna Fail leader Charles Haughey, then in opposition. Again, with Fianna Fail's record in policing partition, what agreement was possible?

During 1988 Gerry Adams and John Hume held lengthy talks. The proposals put forward by Sinn Fein were for a joint approach towards Irish reunification by the SDLP, Fianna Fail and themselves. Not surprisingly the talks collapsed.

At a Sinn Fein conference for its members in the north, held in June 1988, party secretary Tom Hartley produced a document titled 'Broadening the Base'. This argued for 'getting the SDLP to become more republican' by 'dislodging its leadership from its present alliance with imperialism'. During the discussion a Belfast councillor, Mairtin O'Muilleoir, declared: 'We are the only party standing full-square against imperialism—but when it comes to "bins, bodies and bogs" [the usual issues at council meetings] we are only a few degrees to the left of the SDLP.' He added that Sinn Fein's talk of socialism 'was more a case of "fair play for all" than Marxism, more a call for social justice than a battle cry for workers' control.'

In 1986 the Sinn Fein conference had voted to change its policy of not taking any seats it won in the Dublin parliament. The vote was overwhelming, with only a handful of the more conservative delegates walking out in protest. The debate was honest about Sinn Fein's lack of support in the south. One Dublin delegate stated that 'in north inner-city Dublin we are not relevant to the people'. Another delegate said: 'We do not exist in large patches of this country.'

But simply agreeing to take seats in the Dublin parliament would not solve that problem or secure electoral success. In February 1987 a general election was called in the south. Despite the new policy Sinn Fein polled 20,000 fewer votes than in earlier elections for the European parliament. The slippage continued in the June 1989 general election, while there was a significant move leftwards among voters towards the Labour Party and the Workers Party. The Anglo-Irish Agreement had further isolated the struggle in the north while mass unemployment and an employers' offensive in the south had created a more right-wing political climate there. The quest for electoral success meant that Sinn Fein was under pressure to trim its political sails.

From 1987 Charles Haughey of Fianna Fail was in office. A national wages agreement reached with the trade union leaders meant a real cut in workers' wages. Attacks on health spending fuelled a move towards the Labour Party and the Workers Party—but Sinn Fein was marginalised further. The politics of 'pan-nationalism', which appealed for an alliance with the ruling Fianna Fail, offered little way forward for southern workers.

Adams, in a booklet written in 1988 titled **Pathway to Peace**, stated: 'Many of those citizens who form the grassroots membership, or the support base, of most of the political parties in the 26 counties [of southern Ireland] are clearly supportive of Irish unity. The membership of Fianna Fail are obviously sympathetic, even Fine Gael retains its Michael Collins tendency...'

Yet despite much searching amid the grassroots by Sinn Fein, not one branch of Fianna Fail was prepared to take to the streets when Haughey extradited republican prisoners to the north. Indeed opinion polls showed that opposition to the extradition of republicans, far from being concentrated among the grassroots supporters of Fianna Fail, was strongest among those who voted for either the Labour Party or the Workers Party. Support for the ban on republicans being interviewed on the media in the south, on the other hand, came from the upper sections of society, demonstrating a real class divide.

It was not that Sinn Fein appeals to Fianna Fail were simply ineffective. Underlying the Provisionals' strategy was a belief that workers in the south had a common interest with their own ruling class. The argument did not cut with the grain.

Another test for Sinn Fein has been the issue of abortion. The same 1986 conference discussed the issue of abortion. Abortion has always been illegal in the south (in the north it is virtually unobtainable), but the right wing in the Dublin parliament was determined to enshrine this in the constitution. Open support for a woman's right to choose whether to have a child or not was confined largely to the far left (notably the Socialist Workers Movement). Sinn Fein was officially opposed to abortion. It failed to challenge the right-wing Catholic campaign and the anti-abortionists won the vote.

But there was also a strong feminist element within Sinn Fein, which had received encouragement from the leadership. At the 1985 conference they had won a position supporting a woman's right to choose—though this had slipped through at the end of the agenda, and the previous official position also still stood. At the 1986 conference the issue was debated out. A number of activists, most notably women relatives of H-Block prisoners, spoke in support of a woman's right to choose. But the leadership argued against them expressly in terms of the damage that support for abortion was doing to Sinn Fein electorally.

One leadership speaker pointed out that in Fermanagh and South Tyrone they 'were attacked by people on the doorsteps', while another member of the Sinn Fein executive declared that to support a woman's right to choose abortion was a 'propaganda present for our enemies'. Adams himself added that the supporters of a woman's right to choose had 'provoked a reaction' because they 'went too far too fast'. The leadership carried the day.

Even among the supporters of a woman's right to choose there was reluctance to push the issue. One feminist delegate from Derry had explained: 'If we go too far too quickly we'll end up splitting the movement. We could forge ahead with the correct line and lose half our members. That doesn't help Ireland and it wouldn't be totally fair to those people who have been holding the movement together.'

The question of women's rights is fundamental in Ireland. Right-wing religious ideas fasten partition on both sides of the border. To undermine partition these ideas have to be fought. Again in 1986, another referendum to make divorce legal in the south was defeated by the right wing. This time Sinn Fein supported the right to divorce, but in recognition of the 'rights of individual conscience' it stated that its own members were not bound by that position.

Despite the left rhetoric of the Provisionals and Sinn Fein, the limitations are all too clear. In 1983 Danny Morrison's slogan in the European election was: 'One Ireland, one people—the only alternative.' If this is true, then the division between worker and employer in Dublin, Cork or Limerick disappears or becomes secondary. Such political ideas cannot mobilise workers in southern Ireland, who face not the terror of the British army but the all-too-familiar economic attacks of their 'fellow Irish', the employing class.

Nor can such political ideas bridge the sectarian division in the north. When Gerry Adams mentioned unemployment in the manifesto that saw him elected to the Westminster parliament in 1983, it was to talk only of 'nationalist unemployment'. In **An Phoblacht** no effort is made to explain why Protestant workers also suffer from unemployment and bad housing.

To many people the Provisionals' combination of electoralism and militarism seems a contradiction. It isn't. Both are based on elitism—the idea that a dedicated few, either guerrilla fighters or elected representatives, can solve the central problems of society. Neither sees the working class itself—or the people of Northern Ireland—mobilising to achieve their own liberation.

The Provisionals' aim, as they themselves make clear, is not to organise a socialist revolution which would sweep away the system which *created* partition and the poverty which grips Northern Ireland. Instead they limit their aim to ridding Ireland of the border.

The problem remains that, based on a small minority of the population of Ireland, the Provisionals cannot achieve success in even this limited aim. They too are trapped in an *impasse*. The Provisionals were created in opposition to repression. That is why socialists must support them against the British army and the forces of the Northern Ireland state. But their political ideas are too limited to carry that struggle forwards.

Chapter sixteen

Ireland and the struggle for socialism

IRELAND TODAY is a country where the working class is more than two-thirds of the population. Yet the forces on both sides of the border that claim to stand for radical change, and have won a degree of working-class support, rule out any possibility of workers' power. Both these main parties stem from the split in the republican ranks in 1969-70. In the north the Provisionals hold sway among Catholic workers. In the south the Workers Party has increasingly won working-class votes, and seems set to replace the declining Labour Party as the main left-wing party.

But the Provisionals see full Irish independence as their aim. Until then, they say, socialism cannot be achieved. Their leaders argue that in Northern Ireland the class struggle is 'frozen' by the divisions created by partition. So what counts is forcing the British to get out.

The Workers Party also argues that socialism is off the agenda. Instead its leaders say that democratic rule needs to be achieved in the north, while in the south an industrial revolution is needed to transform the economy. Irish capital cannot achieve this, so the Workers Party argues that the European Community and multinational capital must instead carry it through.

Both strategies rest on the 'stages theory'—the idea that a number of separate historical stages have to be passed through before the path is cleared for a socialist transformation. In the here-and-now, objectives must be limited according to what is obtainable in the 'stage' we are supposedly in.

The Provisionals' stress on the national question has ensured their growth in the north, but their failure to mobilise around social issues in the south means their support there is limited. In contrast the Workers Party argues that democratic rule in the north means a return to a Stormont government. They blame the Provisionals for deepening sectarian divisions and today urge support for the RUC and other institutions of the state. Naturally the Workers Party receives little support from Catholic workers in the north—but in the south this is not the case. Since 1982, when they had three MPs elected and held the balance of power in the Irish parliament, they have seemed to offer left-wing policies to Irish workers. They promise to end unemployment and set up better social services.

When the 'troubles' first began in the north in the late 1960s socialists believed this would eventually spill over into an all-Ireland struggle against both partition states. Yet with the exception of the mobilisations after Bloody Sunday in 1972 and around the 1981 hunger strikes, workers in the south have not responded to the struggle of their fellow workers in the Catholic ghettos of the north. Even these two mobilisations centred on expressions of sympathy and support rather than on any recognition of a link between the struggle in the north and the economic and social problems they themselves face in the south.

The idea that the northern troubles would automatically spill over was based on the belief that the south remained in essence a neo-colony of Britain, dominated not politically but economically. But by the 1970s this was no longer true. Irish government figures show that by 1980 70 per cent of new investment in the south was by American multinationals, 21 per cent by European capital, and a mere 4 per cent by British firms —an accurate reflection of Britain's decline as an industrial power. At the beginning of the 1970s Britain provided 70 per cent of the south's imports. By the beginning of the 1980s that had declined to 47 per cent.

In real terms the southern state of Ireland has separate economic interests from those of its British neighbour. This was shown in 1982 when the Irish government publicly broke with Britain, refusing to support Britain's war with Argentina over the Falklands.

Workers in the south do not today confront a state where Britain pulls the real strings of power. They do not confront British-owned firms in their day-to-day struggles over wages and jobs. In this situation simple calls for 'Brits out' do not touch workers in Dublin, Limerick or Cork. Northern Ireland's troubles can seem distant, something for which there appears little explanation or solution.

This does not mean that the tradition of Irish nationalism no longer finds a resonance in the south. It remains part of the national ideology, propagated in the schools and through Gaelic sporting events and upheld by the main political party, Fianna Fail. An opinion poll taken by the **Irish Times** in December 1980 showed 20 per cent of the population agreeing with 'the goal' of the IRA. Yet only 2.8 per cent strongly supported the Provisionals.

The one class which has an interest in destroying the partition states is the Irish working class. Correspondingly the Irish ruling class—on both sides of the border—has an interest in maintaining both the state structures that guarantee their rule and the division of the working class which weakens any movement against that rule. Whatever their respective ideologies and differences of interests, Charles Haughey of Fianna Fail, Alan Dukes of Fine Gael and John Hume of the SDLP share the same overall class interest as Margaret Thatcher, the leaders of the British Labour Party and the Unionists in Northern Ireland.

The British government wishes to end the constant financial drain of policing Northern Ireland. The recession-racked economy of the Northern Ireland state produces no super-profits for British capital.

The Dublin government fears the constant instability of the north. The continuing crisis there, coupled with the south's own economic problems, threatens the stability of Irish capitalism.

The Anglo-Irish Agreement made no attempt to solve the Northern Ireland crisis. Both governments instead see their job as policing that crisis. Even if some sort of power-sharing deal could be reached between the Unionists and the SDLP to re-create some sort of devolved government at Stormont, it would preserve the institutions of the northern state intact. The RUC would remain. So too would the top judges and civil servants who administer Northern Ireland. So too would the slum housing, the unemployment and the sectarian divide.

Traditional Unionist rule may be gone—destroyed by the upsurge of the Catholic working class—and gone for good, but now it is Whitehall that runs the RUC and the UDR, oversees the courts and controls the Northern Ireland economy.

The ruling class in Ireland and Britain cannot simply dismantle the northern state. Its courts, police and administration uphold the rule of capital as they do in any other twentieth-century nation-state. But what the ruling class in Ireland and Britain *can* agree on, wholeheartedly, is an attempt to suppress those who want to destroy that state. The aim of the Anglo-Irish treaty is to increase the isolation of the Provisionals by claiming that real changes can be made and Irish unity is somehow on offer.

Either way, the legacy of British imperialist rule remains. Ireland is a divided country. Sectarianism dominates the northern state. Both north and south unemployment is higher than anywhere else in western Europe. In both states women are denied basic rights.

Since the onset of a new period of world recession the Northern Ireland economy has been in a tail-spin. Factories have shut, investment has dried up and industrial employment has been decimated. Between 1974 and 1985 jobs in manufacturing were cut by almost half. By 1985 64 per cent of the workforce was employed in the service sector (including security!), while manufacturing provided just 19 per cent—a dramatic reversal for an economy traditionally dominated by shipbuilding and heavy engineering.

Since 1938 the Northern Ireland economy has been subsidised by Whitehall. Shorts and Harland and Wolff survive on industrial subsidies that stand at twice those available in the distressed areas of Britain itself. Without these, Northern Ireland's economy would be on a par with that of Argentina. It is a society well and truly in the bankruptcy court.

Despite the south's industrial development it remains dependent on the multinational economy. It has the fourth highest level of debt per head of population of any state in the world—in total this accounts for 150 per cent of its gross national product. In 1986 the central bank reported that £1.5 billion had left the south illegally, avoiding tax, through a 'black hole'. In 1986 a quarter of a million people applied to emigrate to the US, from a country of three and a half million.

Even if Dublin and London could defeat the IRA, which is unlikely, this volcano would erupt again. Capitalism cannot solve the basic problems of Irish society. It cannot even achieve political stability in the north.

Those who pay the price are the working class of Ireland. Whether Protestant or Catholic, whether in Belfast or in Dublin, all suffer from a system in which they have no stake. Partition ensures their division. While that remains true there is no possibility of a socialist state on either side of the border.

The idea that workers, north and south, can be united in a common struggle against both states is, however, no pipe-dream. In the south the working class has a recent history of militancy. In 1964 and 1965 the south actually topped the world strike league. Although it fell to third place in 1966, strikes actually increased by 40 per cent, and 1968 and 1969 saw an explosion of unofficial strikes. Again in the 1970s and early 1980s there was an increase in strikes as the economy entered recession and lay-offs began. Hundreds of thousands of workers struck and marched against the inequality of a tax system which ensured that direct taxation was virtually confined to the working class.

On the other side of the border Northern Ireland still retains a higher level of trade union organisation than Britain. The late 1970s saw Belfast become a centre in the lorry-drivers' and firefighters' strikes against the incomes policy introduced by a British Labour government.

In the 1982 hospitals dispute, when workers demanded decent pay from Thatcher's government, Belfast reached a level of militancy higher than any British city. Shipyard and engineering workers, most of them Protestants, struck in support. Catholic health workers addressed workgate meetings. Protestant workers joined pickets at Belfast's Royal Victoria Hospital—which is on the Catholic Falls Road—and the main day of action saw tens of thousands marching in support of the hospital workers. Even local supermarkets stopped work in solidarity.

Again in 1985 ambulance workers took all-out action over the threat to sell off the service to private contractors. This opened a rash of disputes in the health service.

In the summer of 1986 the strike by civil servants in Northern Ireland offices of the Department of Health and Social Security, against death threats by loyalists against Catholic workers there, was an important lesson: workers in a sectarian state stood together against sectarianism. No doubt this did not automatically lead those Protestant workers who were involved to support the struggle of the Catholic ghettos, but it was a significant step forward. The best workers involved would at least be open to argument.

Throughout 1988 health workers were once again taking action over Thatcher's attacks on their pay and on the health services themselves. And in spring 1989 some 16,000 workers marched against plans to privatise what remains of Harland and Wolff.

Despite this, many on the left and in the Provisionals argue that class unity between Catholic and Protestant workers is not possible. The ideology of sectarianism runs too deep, they say. The divide is too great. They reckon without the ability of workers to change in the course of fighting capitalism. In the heat of struggle, class solidarity can bridge the divide. This can be glimpsed within the mass strikes which shook Belfast in 1907, 1919 and 1944 and in the unemployed riots of 1932. It can be glimpsed in the Dublin lock-out of 1913, the social agitation which developed in the early 1920s and again in the 1960s and 1970s.

The real tragedy of Ireland is the failure to build a powerful socialist movement out of these struggles. The Provisionals reacted to the DHSS workers' strike of 1986 by giving it just one paragraph inside their paper **An Phoblacht**.

Instead the trade union officials, and the Labour politicians who have some influence in the unions, argue that reform can be won. Their consistent cry has been 'Leave it to us!' Let *us* negotiate on your behalf, whether with the employer over wages or the Orange-controlled local council over housing, with the Northern Ireland state over sectarian job discrimination or the British army over harassment, and 'things will change'.

Things haven't changed. The history of the Northern Ireland Labour Party shows that there can be no reforming the sectarian state. In the 1920s, 1940s and 1960s Labour did win support among Protestant workers. It promised change. But when the existence of the state, over which it wished to win control, was itself threatened, it allied with the Unionists time after time. The civil rights movement it eventually denounced as 'divisive'. In 1971 the party had one member in the cabinet that introduced internment. By the end of the 1970s the Northern Ireland Labour Party had ceased to exist. After all, if according to its own argument the state of Northern Ireland had to be maintained, why then should Protestant workers vote Labour when Ian Paisley, Enoch Powell and the Orange Lodge could do the job far better?

Today the Workers Party and trade union officials argue that the solution to sectarianism is to organise workers around 'bread and butter' issues, so as to strengthen union organisation and get left-wingers elected to local councils. To achieve this, they argue, it is necessary *not* to raise issues such as sectarian discrimination and the existence of the border. To do so would upset whatever fragile unity can be achieved.

But these issues *dominate* life in Northern Ireland. The sectarian state and the daily routine of repression cannot be wished away. Workers' unity is impossible if Catholics are debarred from employment in Shorts, for example. Unless the issues are tackled head-on they will always remain to bring divisions between workers.

If socialists are to break the deadlock in Northern Ireland, what arguments must be put forward to win both Protestant and Catholic workers? Workers in Ireland, north and south, have an immediate, shared, common experience. The economic crisis of the past ten years has brought all of them rising unemployment, falling real wages, worsening conditions in all areas of the welfare state—and the failure of reformist trade union leaders and politicians to defend workers from these attacks.

Even in present conditions in Northern Ireland a minority of Protestant workers can be won to see that the state which upholds the divisions between Protestant and Catholic and between north and south is the same state which guarantees unemployment and slum housing for every section of the working class. A minority of Protestant workers, involved in confrontation with the state that is supposedly there to defend their way of life—as hospital workers were in 1982 and ambulance crews in 1985 or 1990—can come to see that that state is an instrument for upholding the rule of the capitalist class and maintaining a divided working class. That understanding can be achieved, not by dropping any mention of partition or the presence of British troops, in an effort to create sham unity, but only by consistently opposing their presence and arguing that they are part of the same system which attacks workers' jobs and living standards.

In struggle that minority can grow.

But in the absence of any organisation which is arguing these things, the situation among Protestant and Catholic workers will remain as it is today.

In the north the main beneficiary of the experience of defeat and demoralisation among Protestant workers has been the hard-line Unionists. Among Catholics it has either been the Provisionals or the SDLP, which continues to attract many workers' votes. Similarly in the south the experience of reformism and the trade union bureaucracy has helped reinforce the position of the ruling class. In the late 1960s the Labour Party grew quickly, promising change. But it then entered three coalition governments with Fine Gael and lost support as a result of helping implement right-wing policies. The trade union leaders have instead sought an alliance with Fianna Fail. In the late 1960s that meant voluntarily accepting crippling restrictions on picketing. In 1988 it meant an agreement to hold down wages.

The majority of Irish workers have voted for Fianna Fail, the 'Green Tories'. In elections in 1989 the smaller left-wing parties, however, gained 22 per cent of the vote. Whatever these parties' reactionary policies regarding the struggle across the border in the north, or their stress that the present system can be used to benefit workers, this shift leftwards represents a step forward. Fewer workers in Ireland today are supporting a nakedly capitalist party. More are recognising, if hesitantly, that the working class has separate class interests from its rulers. More are asking what sort of society they should be striving for.

It is no use appealing to southern workers as fellow Irish men and women to rise up in support of their northern brothers and sisters. It needs to be explained that the struggle in the Catholic working-class ghettos of the Bogside and the Falls Road is the sharp end of a struggle against a system which daily exploits workers in Dublin and Cork. The destruction of the sectarian state of Northern Ireland is not just a matter of fulfilling some nationalist dream. It would mean an end to the partition settlement which guarantees the power of the southern state as well.

Partition serves the interests of the ruling class, north and south of the border. In stark terms, it can be ended only by workers' power, by a struggle in which workers grasp their common interest in ousting the boss class along with the institutions and divisions it has created. Sectarianism will disappear in the process of achieving such a movement.

The argument with the most power to win Protestant workers to action across the sectarian divide would be the existence of a strong working-class movement in the south, fighting not just over jobs and wages, but also to remove the power of the Catholic hierarchy over the state, to win rights such as divorce and contraception, and to remove from power the likes of Garret Fitzgerald and Charles Haughey.

The Provisionals, tragically, cannot meet this task. They offer no perspective for workers who want to develop their own struggles into a challenge to the system. They fail to address Protestant workers in any meaningful terms. In the south they have ducked 'difficult' issues such as abortion, which would have demonstrated true opposition to sectarian divisions.

A new party is needed: a party that is tied neither to reformism nor to the simple quest for Irish unity, a party that focuses on the struggles of workers themselves, a party which seeks to develop these struggles into a challenge to the capitalist system itself. In short, a party whose perspective is *revolutionary* change.

The crucial battle is not fought with bombs and guns. It is a battle of *ideas*, the struggle to break the hold of the past, the conservative traditions that weigh down the majority of workers. But this isn't a battle which centres just on meetings and abstract propaganda. It centres instead on the daily struggle in the workplace, the daily struggle against the foreman, the boss and ultimately the employing class itself, the struggle in which workers transcend their own passivity and can be won to revolutionary ideas, to socialism and workers' power.

In Ireland today that battle of ideas is very real.

Throughout Ireland the backward ideas of Fianna Fail, Ian Paisley and the Catholic church have great influence. But the states where these ideas rule are also in deep crisis. In the south the Dublin government faces crippling foreign debts, which swallow most of the revenue from taxation. In the north the old Unionist Party has splintered. Mounting redundancies and falling standards of living have undermined the confidence of Protestant workers in the benefits of the system. In the south unemployment is the highest of any country in Europe. In the north it is higher still, topping 20 per cent. In the Catholic areas of West Belfast it is over 50 per cent.

In this situation, where workers look to Fianna Fail or the Workers Party, to Gerry Adams or Ian Paisley, the ideas of revolutionary socialism may seem marginal. Yet historical evidence has shown how, in times of crisis, such ideas can suddenly seize the imaginations of millions of workers and find themselves at the centre of events.

In Ireland today few on the left accept the need for such a revolutionary socialist party. Many are attracted towards the Workers Party. Even more look towards the Provisionals. But so long as the struggle of Catholic workers remains trapped in the ghettos the deadlock which grips the struggle in Northern Ireland will continue.

Sectarianism and partition are products of capitalism's 'solution' to its Irish problem. The two states created in 1921 guaranteed that the Irish ruling class would maintain its control. The two states hang together. If sectarianism and partition are to be brought to an end, then *both* states must be removed. The key to this lies both north and south of the border: as in any other country in the world the key division in Ireland today is one of class, between the employing class and the working class.

In 1902 James Connolly told an audience of Irish-Americans in New York:

> I represent only the class to which I belong and that is the working class. The Irish people, like the people of this and other capitalist countries, are divided into the master class and the working class, and I could not represent the entire Irish people on the account of the antagonistic interests of these classes.

Socialists oppose the presence of British troops in Northern Ireland. We support those who resist them. But because we follow James Connolly in recognising the division of the Irish people along class lines, we argue that only one class has an interest in ending the partition of Ireland: the working class.

Suggested further reading

James Connolly's **Labour in Irish History** is still the best account and analysis of Ireland's history. It is available as a Bookmarks Revolutionary Classic with an introduction by Kieran Allen. Connolly's **Selected Writings** are also worth reading; there are several editions available. Another good socialist history of Ireland is T A Jackson's **Ireland her own**.

The best description of the origins of the troubles of the past 20 years is the hugely enjoyable **War in an Irish Town** by Eamonn McCann, while Michael Farrell's **The Orange State** is the best available history of Northern Ireland. George Dangerfield's **The Damnable Question** traces events from the fall of Parnell to partition. The period since then is covered in detail in **Northern Ireland: The political economy of conflict**, by Bob Rowthorn and Naomi Wayne. The argument for the withdrawal of British troops from the north is most forcefully put by Paul Foot in **Ireland: Why Britain must get out**.

C Desmond Greaves' **The Life and Times of James Connolly** is a useful examination of the life and ideas of this great revolutionary socialist. There is a further book on Connolly, by Kieran Allen, in the final stages of publications as this book goes to press. For anyone wanting to study the Irish left after Connolly's execution Mike Milotte's **Communism in Modern Ireland** gives a wealth of information. The political position put forward by Sinn Fein today is examined and countered by Kieran Allen in his pamphlet **Is southern Ireland a neo-colony?**

Finally, John Gray's study of the 1907 Belfast general strike, **City in Revolt**, provides a picture of the working class of that city, while Ronnie Munck and Bill Rolston's **Belfast in the 1930s**, despite its academic sections, provides a wealth of background.

Other publications from Bookmarks

Labour in Irish history / *James Connolly*
Written as a challenge to the Irish nationalists in whose company Connolly
was later to fight and die, this book is the classic analysis of the role of the
working class in the struggle for Irish freedom. *£2.95 / US$4.95*

Is southern Ireland a neo-colony? / *Kieran Allen*
A critique of the politics of Sinn Fein, showing how their emphasis on the
national question works against the interests of the Irish working class.
£1.50 / US$2.50

The Labour Party: A Marxist history / *Tony Cliff and Donny Gluckstein*
A history of the Labour Party which measures it against its own pretensions
as standard-bearer of the working class, tracing its path from birth to the
crisis of the 1980s. *£7.95 / US$13.50*

1919: Britain on the brink of revolution / *Chanie Rosenberg*
The year 1919 was a watershed in British politics: one civil servant said
afterwards: 'I do not think at any time in our history since the Bristol riots
we have been so near revolution.' *£2.25 / US$4.50*

Intifada / *Phil Marshall*
Following the mass uprising of Palestinians in Israel's occupied territories,
this book exposes the structure of domination of which Israel is a
keystone—and which oppresses the whole of the Middle East.
£5.95 / US$11.00

Sex, class and socialism / *Lindsey German*
What is the source of women's oppression? This book offers a Marxist
analysis of the relationship between capitalism, the family and women's
oppression—and an alternative to feminism. *£5.95 / US$11.00*

Class struggles in Eastern Europe 1945-83 / *Chris Harman*
Gorbachev was not the first to attempt reform in the Eastern bloc: this
book gives a vivid account of struggles ranging from Hungary 1956 to
Poland 1981, with particular emphasis on the role of the workers—on
whose shoulders the hopes of the 1990s rest. *£7.95 / US$13.50*

The fire last time: 1968 and after / *Chris Harman*
The year 1968 was a political watershed: the May events in France, the
Prague Spring in Czechoslovakia, ghetto risings in the USA. This book
examines the contradictions in the world system which led to these
upheavals—and how the system reasserted its control. *£6.95 / US$13.50*

The Quiet Revolutionary / *The autobiography of Margaret Dewar*
From schoolgirl in Petrograd during the 1917 revolution to become an
opponent of both Stalinism and Nazism in the Germany of the 1930s—this
is the story of one of the 'ordinary' people who are the real movers of
history. *£5.95 / US$12.50*

Russia: From workers' state to state capitalism
/ *Peter Binns, Tony Cliff and Chris Harman*
An analysis of the process which followed the Russian revolution of 1917,
by which the vitality of workers' power—whose aim was socialism—was
turned into the suffocating rule of a bureaucracy whose aim was a new
state-controlled capitalism. *£2.50 / US$4.75*

Revolution and counter-revolution in Iran / *Phil Marshall*
From the oppression of the Shah to that os the Ayatollah—but why?
This book looks at the various forces acting during the Iranian revolution of
1979, particularly the working class and the left. *£3.50 / US$6.75*

South Africa between reform and revolution / *Alex Callinicos*
The crisis of white rule in South Africa has been at the centre of world
attention since the popular upsurge of 1984. Only swingeing emergency
powers hold the regime in place. This analysis looks at the strengths and
weaknesses of both sides. *£4.95 / US$8.50*

All available from bookshops, or by post (add 10 per cent for postage) from

BOOKMARKS
265 Seven Sisters Road, London N4 2DE, England
PO Box 16085, Chicago, IL 60616, USA
GPO Box 1473N, Melbourne 3001, Australia